BREAK
THE GRIP
OF PAST
LOVERS

BREAK THE GRIP OF PAST LOVERS

Reclaim Your Personal Power

Recover from Neglect,
Manipulation, or Betrayal

Reawaken Your Emotional Intimacy

JUMANA SOPHIA

Hierophant publishing

Cover design by Laura Beers
Cover image by seewhatmitchsee/gettyimages
Interior design by Frame25 Productions

Hierophant Publishing
www.hierophantpublishing.com

Library of Congress Control Number: 2019944241

ISBN: 978-1-938289-95-8

Dedicated to all women who find the courage to claim love and sexuality as a sacred path.

*Sexual embodiment and integrity does not
ask us to become something we are not.
It asks us to become ourselves, fully.*
—Sarah Byrden, The Great Remembering

Contents

Introduction

What's the difference between a friend and a lover?
Sex.

The distinction is so simple, yet we often don't consider all that it entails.

Past lovers, whether they were with you for a night or for decades, leave impressions that can linger long after the relationship is over—and in many cases dramatically affect your self-esteem, your capacity for future intimacy, and your emotional well-being. Whether we like it or not, there is rarely, if ever, such a thing as casual sex.

In the current cultural climate, where sexual relationships swing between careless impulse and overly moralized repression, our society has lost the pulse of what truly healthy and vibrant female sexuality is. We no longer know what to do when a sexual relationship falls apart, leaving the wreckage of betrayal, abandonment, neglect, or even abuse in its wake. So many women are suffering—from mild discomfort to full-blown anxiety, from depression to total sexual shutdown; from desperate loneliness to recklessly empty promiscuity.

As women we are capable of so much more, but we are rarely, if ever, shown the way.

Female sexuality is a unique weave of physical energy, emotional connection, mental engagement, and spiritual communion. Sadly, this weave has been ignored, invalidated, or even demonized by much of our society over time. As a result, the mysteries of female sexuality are buried under mountains of oversexualized cultural patterning, dismissal of the rich heritage of deep feminine reverence and power, and ignorance of the vast inner terrain that lives within women.

In simple terms, this means that female sexuality is both powerful and vulnerable, and it is unique in a way that almost all healing modalities, therapies, religions, and even spiritual paths don't fully recognize. For as necessary and potent as such practices can be, they have gaps in their understanding about some very core concepts related to women. Those gaps become unbridgeable chasms when it comes to reclaiming our female sexuality, caring for that nature, and understanding and clearing lingering sexual experiences.

If you are like so many of the women I work with, you picked up this book because you are carrying heartache, grief, pain, and unmet longing—all of which can be traced back to one or more past loverships. These experiences may also have resulted in the formation of sexual habits that don't fulfill your deepest needs, such as shutting down your sexuality, or overgiving to your partner. For so many of us, after enough heartbreak and disappointment, the desire to love deeply, securely, passionately, and with integrity ends up either dimmed almost to extinction or enflamed with a frustrated anger that burns almost everything it touches.

We must remember and honor the fact that we were created to be sexual creatures, freed from the pendulum swing of oppression and reaction to that oppression. Liberated from all that push and pull, we have the opportunity to recover and know the radical truth, wisdom, and sexual wholeness that is our birthright. This is not a cultural, social, or personality-based liberation. This is a recovery of deep feminine power and knowledge that will free you regardless of circumstance.

Think of "breaking the grip of past lovers" as code for freeing yourself of deeply unconscious limitations and misunderstandings you have inherited about what it means to be a woman—particularly a woman of sexual desire, longings, emotion, and passion. The breaking free process will require you to be more vulnerable and more sensitive with yourself. The good news is that the freedom that awaits you is vastly more powerful and healing than you can imagine.

My Story

In my case, the journey to shed the residual impact of past lovers was not a well-intentioned choice toward self-improvement. It was a necessity born of devastation.

When I was in my mid-thirties, my marriage of seven years (my second), was falling apart. After enduring multiple betrayals, I had accumulated a convincing distrust of intimacy—both with my husband and with anyone else I might be romantically close to after that. I was lost inside a tangle of grief, depression, longing, and isolation that was coloring everything, stealing the passion from my life, and relegating me to the kind of subtle despair and unmet longing that I had witnessed in so many other women. I was exhausted from the pressure of single motherhood and shattered by the experience of witnessing what had once been touching love devolve into chaos, dishonesty, and heartbreak.

Despite all of this—and because I didn't want to lose the relationship we had built, because I was afraid of being financially on my own, and mostly because I came to deeply feel that receiving his full attention and sexual fidelity was how I would feel whole again—I ended up staying despite my partner sustaining an intimate dynamic that eroded my sense of self, my trust in men in general, and my hope of ever finding a full and honoring sexuality. As a result of that relationship, I shut down emotionally and sexually. I became jealous and paranoid. And I came to believe that I was not (nor would I ever be) "woman enough."

I also lost important time and presence with my son in his younger years because I was emotionally distracted. I got further and further from my own sense of my beauty, my worth, my fullness, and my pleasure. I had panic attacks most nights, and significant depression. I can remember countless experiences of finding myself crumpled up on the floor crying, fighting, in desperate emotional pain. And then the terrible confusion created by all of our "good" times, when I would remember how much we loved each other and believe again that we could make it . . . only to be shattered by more dishonesty. On top of it all, I was so deeply ashamed and humiliated by what was going on in our relationship that I hid the truth from all of my friends. They would have loved and supported me, but in my state I could only imagine feeling humiliated and exposed. So I isolated myself from their support and fell even deeper into my sense of unworthiness. I was so desperate for the relationship to work out that I was hiding the truth from anyone who might call it what it was and hold me accountable to either radically change or to be brave enough to leave the dysfunction that I was tolerating.

Before this unhealthy dynamic, I had generally felt very nourished by my sexuality. Not perfect, by any means, but I had come to a place in my life and my sexual expression where I was free of insecurities that had plagued my younger years. Yet by the time I finally ended our marriage, I felt fractured and unworthy of love or fidelity. My light had dimmed, and I was deeply suffering from maintaining and allowing an intimate relationship that was very much in opposition to my core values.

My pain and shame, mixed with an almost forgotten hope that I would one day have the kind of honoring and passionate intimate relationship I deserved, led me to explore esoteric teachings on the sacred nature of female sexuality. I fell in love with what I found, and over a period of years I walked myself through the disentangling of my relationship and the restoration of my deep feminine nature. It was then that I began a commitment to personal cultivation practices in this area that continues to this day.

Because of the transformation I experienced, I began teaching and supporting other women to do the same, and, lo and behold, I discovered an unspoken epidemic of unresolved intimacies that most women were just tolerating or muddling through. It was stunning how similar our stories were, how devastating and confusing past sexual relationships continued to be, and how much we were all feeling compromised, stuck and lost to ourselves, sometimes years after a relationship had ended. What I learned in my own journey and from helping other women recover is what you will find in the pages that followed.

When I look back now, after metabolizing the residual impact of my past lovership and recovering my sense of self, I see that what I experienced was a type of initiation. It was not one I would have ever chosen, but it was one that taught me the importance of honoring my personal power and committing to never relinquishing my sexual sovereignty to the control of someone else again.

In one sense, my failed relationship had cost me a version of innocence. But as I moved through the initiation, I gained a state of personal power that now never leaves me. It was as if losing my power and reclaiming it were necessary steps on the journey to true sovereignty.

The gifts of this, including a present relationship that meets me in my values and takes them even further, have been abundant in all aspects of my life. I would never say it was an easy road, as I spent years feeling lost before finding my way back home, but as I moved through the initiation and stayed committed to it, not only did I clear all residual impact of my past loverships, but I discovered that finding my freedom gifted me the ability to hold reverence and respect for myself regardless of the circumstances that may arise.

Your Story

As you consider what you have experienced in past relationships, can you sense a golden thread of initiation running throughout them, no matter however difficult they may have been? For instance, on the other side of betrayal may be the gift that you will never again betray *yourself*. On the other side of neglect may be your commitment to never again neglect your own essence. On the other side of manipulation may be a radical cultivation of discernment that will never again let you ignore your intuition when it signals that something isn't right or you are not safe.

I invite you to take a moment—let the costs of past relationship choices serve as fuel for your commitments to what you will choose now and how you will advocate for yourself so that you never lose power like that again. Initiations born of past loverships change us forever, but the full fruit of these is greater love, greater power, and a fierce commitment to our own feminine essence. In my experience, this type of self-commitment actually *needed* an initiation born of loss and challenge in order to fully evolve. When you complete this type of initiation, you become a sword so tempered by the fire of life's passages that you cut through any habit of self-rejection and become the greatest friend and ally you have ever known.

You have a life to live, love to share, children to raise, pleasure to experience, and so many gifts still to explore, but if you haven't cleared the residual impact of past lovers, you are losing time, energy, power, and joy. Tens of thousands of women have now worked with the process in this book, and their stories are full of hope and full of compassion for themselves, for their past lovers, and for you as a woman who must also find her way through the tangled devastation of a broken sexual relationship. They are healing fully and finally from emotional neglect, betrayal, infidelity, mistreatment, and vicious manipulation, and so can you.

No matter how bleak or stuck you feel when you think about your past lovership or how deep the cost of a past relationship may have been, there is some part of you that can and will create pure gold from the anguish of it all. This is the spirit of a queen who knows her worth, and who has matured through hardship into a woman who will never abandon her throne again.

This is what you were always meant to be and what you are destined to become. You are both powerful and vulnerable, and by reclaiming both your beauty and your pain, you will free yourself to know more of your own happiness, fulfillment, peace, and pleasure than the world has told you is possible. As women of these times, we are turning the tide from habitual dysfunction to grace-filled empowerment, from collective amnesia to full remembrance of our own mysteries. I am honored to be on this journey of liberation with you. So let us begin . . .

ONE

The Journey to Wholeness

A dear friend of mine has a small ceramic cup that is very special to her. Years ago, it slipped from her hands in the sink and a piece of it broke off. As she went to discard the cup with a heavy heart, she remembered hearing something about an ancient Japanese art called *kintsugi*—the practice of mending broken pottery with golden lacquer. In this process, the brokenness of an item becomes a highlight, an artful aesthetic addition as well as a practical fix. The resulting piece is even more beautiful, and this is what she did with this cup, which now sits proudly on display in her kitchen.

This story moved me deeply, as I understood it as a symbol for the transformation that is available to us all. When we are broken, we might feel inclined to hide the wound or try to get back to the way we were before. But rather than seeking to be "like new," we can aim to become whole again—our broken histories incorporated into our beauty.

The experience of sexual intimacy with another person can be transformative, in that it can shape and change us in profound ways. For this reason, experiences of past lovers—particularly those that ruptured, confused, distorted, or diminished you—have an ongoing impact on your whole being.

As I mentioned in the introduction, there is rarely, if ever, a sexual exchange that is truly casual. After all, you are opening up the deepest private place in your being to another, whether for a night or a lifetime. The experience you have with a lover can open you up to both immense beauty and intense suffering. The power of these feelings is in direct relation to the potential and depth of your sexual being.

In a perfect world, we would have a clear process for handling the loss of an intimate relationship. We would live in a culture that acknowledged the energetic reality of being entwined with another person, and we would be taught how to untangle or unwind what no longer served us as relationships fall apart. We would have the time to mourn, to restore, to recalibrate. We would have support through this powerful life transition, rather than being told it was something to just move past.

Of course, this is not the case in our society. Instead, when a relationship ends—especially if things such as neglect, manipulation, or betrayal are involved—we often struggle with a lack of clarity about how to move forward through the wreckage. When we add the pressures of our jobs, taking care of family, or other large commitments, the struggle to keep it all going can feel overwhelming and leave us longing for even a glimpse of support or release.

This is exhausting and leaves a lot of unclear agreements and tangled energies between you and your former partner. Even when we part ways with a lover with good communication and well-wishes, there will often be a period of mourning, adjustment, and emotional transition that demands its full time and space.

As we move through the work in this book, we will dig into the heap of your past loverships and harvest the gold that remains there. With this rediscovered gold, we will fashion a crown of self-authority for your brow. Together, we will realign with wholeness, power, and the truth of the female sexual current that flows through us all—vulnerable and deeply sensitive, the most generative, creative force on the planet.

In the many years I have helped women in this arena, I have found that even in the most extreme cases of abuse and neglect, you can *always* transform a toxic experience into energy that sustains and strengthens you. I have witnessed time and time again that women have unparalleled capacities for transformation. This is the balance of power and vulnerability of being a woman, of what it is to open so deeply to another.

While difficult or traumatic experiences can be addressed to some extent through therapy, along with the wisdom of time, the support of friends, and even the arrival of a new and better-suited lover, these things are just a temporary bandage on a deep wound. Healing the female sexual current and connecting with a deep knowing of oneself as a woman of value and wholeness requires a different approach. That's because, at the deepest level, the rupture of previous intimacies usually results in a rift between you and your trust in yourself, your belief in your own worth and goodness.

The good news is that there is an ancient and interrupted lineage of women's wisdom that offers active arts of recovery and restoration. These arts have been lost or hidden at times in our collective history, and we have all paid the price. The approach gathered in these pages is an accumulation of these arts; this book serves as a guide for restoring healthy sexuality, discernment, and openness to your intimate life.

As you shed the residual impact of past lovers and start tending to the rich emotional terrain within you, you will open on every level, blossoming into aspects of life and yourself that are beyond imagining. The journey in the following pages will change the very fabric of your being, not just your ideas or perceptions about yourself or your relationships. When you put past loverships fully to rest, you come home to yourself, and you enter a state of balance and wholeness that you may never have known, even before your sexual adventures (or misadventures, as you might see them now).

Here are the goals I'd like you to achieve by the end of our journey together:

♥ Reclaim your personal power.

- Restore uncompromising self-respect.

- Celebrate the things about yourself as a woman and a lover that you used to view with criticism.

- Prepare to receive a new lover or your current lover with greater emotional intimacy.

- Become more expansive and confident sexually.

- Experience a deeper trust and love with yourself and your current or future partner.

This is a big list, and I have witnessed many, many women claim every one of these gifts. I want you to do the same. Are you ready?

Begin Where You Are

You may not yet realize the extent to which past loverships can color your sense of self, dim your radiance, and block your ability to be truly intimate with yourself and another. Thankfully, the heartbeat of your feminine power is much deeper and more powerful. Under no circumstances can it be conquered by these experiences. They have affected you, and it is important to know how, but it's you who will determine the ultimate outcome of these experiences. In fact, you will use these very experiences to tap into a power within you that will return you to your essence.

Pause with me to consider these possible indicators that residual trauma or experiences of past lovers still have you in their grip:

- ♥ Low self-esteem and/or low self-respect

- ♥ Mistrust in the world and/or relationship partners

- ♥ A general feeling of insecurity in your relationships

- ♥ Inability to trust yourself to make good choices

- ♥ Denial/denigration of your emotional needs and deepest desires in a relationship

- ♥ Sexual stagnancy (you have become cut off from your sexual vitality) or a tendency to ignore your healthy sexual boundaries (you give yourself away)

- ♥ Consistent recreation of abusive or negligent relationship patterns

- ♥ Inability to receive or trust the love and intimacy that is truly being held for you by a trustworthy and respectful partner

Too often, we tolerate many of these states of being, thinking this is "just the way it is." We create stories about ourselves that support these ideas, and we often criticize ourselves for not being stronger, more confident, clearer, freer, and more alive. We might even blame ourselves for being on the receiving end of bad behavior from others.

It's certainly not easy to transform and harvest strength from the devastation that ruptured intimacies can bring. It takes work. But through clearing, healing, and recovering your power from these experiences, you can embrace a transformation that will lead you to a healthy sexuality, unrelenting self-confidence, and right relationship with yourself and another. As you reclaim your wholeness, you'll find yourself unable to betray your own trust or your own best interests ever again. In that way, your past failed relationships will become fuel for the flame of your current desires, and you'll see them as some of the most important and necessary experiences of your life. This is true regardless of your age, your past, or your perceived limitations.

When past intimacies remain unresolved—when they block the full embodiment of your sexuality and your ability to foster intimacies with another—the cost to you and to those you love extends far beyond the bedroom. A woman who is nourished and honored by the intimacies she chooses will flower and bear fruit to all in her sphere. A woman who is diminished, compromised, or entrapped by the intimacies she chooses often can't fully show up in the other areas of her life until the remnants of the past are cleared.

As we begin this journey together, please remember that it's not your fault if you've found yourself unable to let go of a person, a pattern, a past, or a compromised perception of yourself. It's simply that you're navigating difficult terrain without the necessary tools or maps to guide you home. We're going to change all that here. You'll be amazed by what you really are, what you are truly capable of, and how much life there is just on the other side of what may seem like an insurmountable hill.

You deserve a relationship that is respectful and fulfilling on all levels. It serves nothing and no one for you to settle for less, to surrender to feeling dimmed and shut down, or to offer the pearls of your intimacy to anyone who cannot cherish their value. I commend you for taking the time to free yourself from the grip of past lovers and clear the distortions you may have picked up along the way. This is one of the greatest gifts you can give to yourself and everyone who enters your world.

I have been there myself, and I am grateful on behalf of all the beings who make up your world that you are tending to the sensitive and unspeakable miracle that is you. It takes courage to pick up this book, to embrace this journey of empowerment and transformation, to get radically honest with yourself, and to take a clear look at what has been in order to shift into what will be. It takes self-respect to steward your needs, to honor your intimate terrain, to care for your heart, and to heal what has been hurt in you. No one else can do this for you; this is a journey you must take for yourself.

I am here with you in spirit, and by the end of this journey you will be in a deeper, more beautiful, and more truthful understanding of who you really are as a woman, regardless of what circumstances or past loverships have led you to believe. You are vulnerable and powerful beyond your imagining.

Rituals

On our journey together I will recommend a handful of simple rituals, all of which are designed to help you break the grip of past lovers, step into your own personal power, and claim your sexual sovereignty. Before we go further, I'd like to say a few words about rituals in general, because too often (in part due to religious backgrounds or an avoidance of the superstitious) women will avoid ritual because they misunderstand the power and point of it.

The deepest power of ritual comes from two things:

- ♥ Your choice and focus

- ♥ Your connection with your subconscious

Ritual focuses your attention on the transformation you're experiencing, and helps you clarify your intentions. The simple act of turning toward yourself and your desire for transformation with more than just your thinking mind activates a change deep inside your being. This outer manifestation of an inward desire creates an energetic wave that is far more powerful than just the ritual itself might appear to be.

If clearing past lovers and integrating major sexual experiences were as simple as consciously choosing to do it, we'd all have done it (and a whole bunch of other challenging things) long ago. It's obvious that sexuality impacts us on levels far deeper than the conscious mind and is profoundly mysterious. Ritual actions, even simple ones such as lighting a candle, creating a beautiful altar, or washing or burning things to purify them, can help you connect to the deeper aspects of your being, in an easy, personal way.

Remember, you cannot connect with the subconscious, or the mysteries within you, through the conscious mind. The conscious mind speaks in linear terms, understanding cause and effect through analysis. Of course it's important to care for and enlist the power of your conscious mind, and you can do so through therapy, talking, and other such processes. But with the subconscious, you have to use a whole different approach. The subconscious is affected through symbols, action, and sensory realities like taste, color, touch, and sound. When you practice a personal ritual, what you're really doing is making a connection with the part of yourself that you can't know consciously. You are speaking to a deep aspect of yourself that can't be spoken to with simple, linear words. It's this deeper, more mysterious, and hidden part of you that often holds on to unresolved experiences.

Creating a ritual does not have to be in conflict with anything else in your life—your religious background or your family or cultural beliefs. In fact, creating personal rituals is all about incorporating these things, or anything that is personally meaningful to you, into the ritual itself. Knowing this, as we go forward explore the power of ritual to bring your subconscious into alignment with your conscious desires.

Action Steps

To set the stage for this journey, I invite you to choose a journal just for the purpose of working through this book. This will be the first ritual you implement, and I encourage you to either write or reflect on past writings two to three times per week to start. Setting time aside to write and to think will not only help you integrate the lessons in this book, but will also help you gain clarity on past experiences and the direction you want to take in the future.

Journaling

Below are some of the questions posed in this chapter. Take a moment now to write the answers in your journal. Magic occurs when we write down these answers rather than just think about them, as we will often see patterns on the page that we don't notice in our thoughts. For that reason, I encourage you to be as specific as possible.

This is for your eyes only, so write fully and freely, without editing yourself or beating yourself up. I encourage you to be gentle with yourself in this process, as it may bring up strong emotions and troubling memories. That's okay. Through these questions, we are simply beginning the process of you getting to know yourself—exactly as you are, right this moment.

I have included some examples to get you started.

1. In past relationships, what has been the cost to you of relinquishing your needs?

> *Example:* In my marriage, I lost sight of my need to spend time by myself. This cost me the ability to renew myself as an introvert and led me to push through my discomfort until it caught up with me and I got resentful.

> *Example:* I have a deep need for secure attachment, a commitment that I can trust. I relinquished that need thinking that I

could grow by being more "adventurous" and "open," and it resulted in irreconcilable feelings of insecurity and anxiety that eventually soured the relationship.

Example: I am a social, extroverted person who thrives on interaction. Because of my partner's jealousy, I stopped going out and seeing friends, dancing, and doing all the things I love. It cost me joy and my sense of freedom.

2. When have you compromised on things that were previously nonnegotiable?

Example: Cheating was nonnegotiable, but I allowed myself to be talked into another chance after it happened.

Example: Due to past painful relationships with addicts and my own addictive tendencies, it was nonnegotiable that my partner maintain his sobriety. I allowed myself to be convinced that it wasn't my right to ask him to stop when he started a daily drink, but it created a backslide in my life that almost cost me my sobriety.

Example: Being a single parent in charge of the loving guidance of my kids was nonnegotiable; I am the final say when it comes to limits and consequences. I compromised in order to keep the peace, and my relationship with my kids suffered.

3. When have you bowed your head and turned your eyes away so that you would not see what you didn't want to see?

Example: I didn't want to see the manipulation and jealousy that was keeping me from having a closer relationship with my siblings.

Example: I didn't want to see that my husband was actually emotionally and mentally unstable, because I knew it would mean that he didn't actually have the capacity to have a healthy relationship with me.

Example: I didn't want to hear that my partner wasn't actually ready for a commitment because I wanted a relationship so badly. I leaned way out of my center and did everything I could to keep him happy so that I wouldn't have to acknowledge that he never felt ready to have this relationship in the first place.

4. How many times have you stayed in a relationship, or not spoken your truth in one, out of fear of the consequences?

Example: I felt I wasn't lovable enough to ever have another relationship, so I stayed and kept quiet, thinking that this was the best I could do.

Example: I was convinced that I could never survive financially on my own, so I stayed and endured his neglect and disinterest rather than risk losing financial stability.

Example: I pretended not to know about his affair because of the children, because I was afraid that it would end the relationship and I would lose the family bond we had created.

Next, I'd like you to review the list that follows. Which of the following experiences of ruptured intimacy are part of your own history? Which of these experiences have defined or destroyed intimacies in your life? Which still echo in your heart and cage your spirit? In your journal, write down the details of any experience you had from the list below and how it has affected you.

1. Neglect

Example: After a long day of work and being apart, instead of turning toward me to share the day or simple wordless intimacy, he would immediately turn to the TV and tune me out. Requests for attention or intimacy from me were met with frustration and judgment.

2. Betrayal

Example: I asked for months if the jealous, insecure feeling I was having about his coworker had any truth to it. He claimed again and again that there was nothing going on and accused me of being crazy and possessive. When the truth came to light that he had been having an affair all that time, I had to come to terms with the web of lies I had been caught in.

3. Manipulation

Example: She claimed to want a conscious, loving relationship, but every time I expressed a need or made a request she would turn it on me immediately, calling me names, digging at my deepest vulnerabilities, and threatening to leave if I didn't stop being so "needy."

4. Sexual and/or emotional insensitivity

Example: When he wanted sex, he would guilt me into going to bed with him, regardless of what I was feeling. After we made love, he would simply turn over and fall asleep.

5. Physical and/or emotional abandonment

Example: Whenever strong feelings would arise in me, whether tears or anger or deep worries, rather than reaching out to hold me or be by my side, he would change the subject, criticize my "excessive emotionality," or just leave the room.

6. Violation of trust

Example: She lied to me about big and small things. When I shared my deepest vulnerabilities with her, she used them as ammunition against me.

7. Criticism

Example: Nothing was ever quite right, quite enough. He would make cutting comments that made me feel self-conscious, especially when I was naked in front of him. I never felt confident, relaxed, or beautiful just as I was.

One of the reasons many of us stay paralyzed by past relationships is because of that unresolvable feeling that the cost was so great—that we lost months or years to something that was neither honoring nor honest. We believe that it's too late for us; we can never get that time, that love, that wholeness back again. We should have known better. We feel shame at allowing or even participating in long-term dynamics of negligence, control, criticism, and dishonesty. If this has happened in more than one past lovership (which is common), we wonder how broken we must be to keep attracting and creating the same pain over and over again.

Of all these negative ideas, perhaps the most dangerous is an internalized, often invisible, belief about being broken. Brokenness makes you a stranger to your true nature and contributes to losing faith in your power and potential to have trustworthy, loving, and respectful intimacies.

I want to be clear about something before we go any further: you are not broken. Look over what you have written in your journal. Love wants to know you as you are. You will be stronger as a result of this, and you will know a deeper love with a respectful partner because of it.

Personal Power

Think of a powerful river, flowing through a deep valley. You can build a dam to harness and divert the energy of the rushing water, but not without a cascade of consequences. The resulting upstream flood can destroy natural habitats, while the lack of flow downstream can interrupt the life cycles of fish and amphibians. The river itself may break through or flow around the dam, causing destruction with the release of too much power all at once. Just so, your personal power has a natural state, and any blockages of energy can have profound unintended consequences.

In order to completely release the residual impact of past lovers, once and for all, you will need to reclaim what I call your *personal power*. What does this mean? Personal power is that sense of self that endures regardless of circumstance—one that provides you with a trustworthy discernment about what is or is not good for you, if only you will listen. This is not the power you derive from ego or accomplishment or from feeling control or dominance over someone or something. Your personal power connects you to your deepest desires and guides you toward your highest good.

When your personal power is intact, you will naturally prioritize the health and vibrancy of your own well-being over all other things, including the attitudes of your partner, the maintenance of a partnership that doesn't serve you, and your own investment in not seeing what you don't want to see. The idea of fully embracing your personal power might be intimidating; it's not always going to be easy to listen to your inner voice and follow its guidance. If you are not yet comfortable owning your wholeness, it might not even feel *possible* to embrace your personal power. How can you ever be led by some kind of complete inner wisdom if you don't feel like you're enough? This is one of the many reasons you may have given away personal power to a partner or relationship in the past.

In fact, one of the most fundamental reasons that a past lover or relationship remains difficult for you to put down, even into the present moment, is because of the dynamic of power loss that occurred as a result. The manifestations that occur from this loss of personal power in a relationship—or when struggling to heal from a relationship—are numerous and can include anxiety, confusion, depression, obsessive thinking, rigidity, helpless rage, and self-doubt.

In all of these instances, the underlying belief was that you were not enough and your former lover(s) had, knew, or were something that you desperately needed to be whole. For so many of us, this belief is visceral and affects our emotional health and our behavior, and it can even appear in our dreams. This belief runs deep. Even if you can rationally spot the fallacy and understand the dynamics behind it, that knowledge alone won't recover the power you have surrendered. For this reason, you may have moments of breakthrough, understanding, or mental clarity, only to find yourself back in the same cycle of emotional entanglement days or weeks later. Cognitive understanding is important, but it takes more to fully set yourself free.

Clearing the Energy of Past Lovers

In my personal experience, and in my work with thousands of other women, in order for your personal power restoration to be effective, you need to clear the energies of these relationships—not just the thoughts or perceptions in your mind. Energetic work is difficult to describe in words because its very nature is to go beyond what is verbal and literal. As we go through this process of restoring power in the coming chapters, I invite you to try to *feel into* the concepts of personal power and energy rather than just think about them. This means taking note of your emotional state throughout the day and feeling your body sensations as you work. These are clues that will help you know more about what is happening with the energy of past lovers as you clear it.

Retrieving the personal power that was lost in the breakdown of past loverships requires this very different approach. Sexual relationships are so much more than just rational experiences; they are born in passion, magnetism, feeling, archetype, desire, and instinct. When it's time to put a sexual relationship to rest, it must be resolved in those areas as well. All the mental analysis and positive belief systems in the world can't stand up to the subconscious energy and emotion that must be healed and made whole in you.

Many of us have ventured into talk therapy to heal, and while analyzing and discussing can offer vast relief, it leaves much undone. When you adventure in the field of sexuality, you evoke power and vulnerability *inside of an energetic weave with another person*. This is not simply psychological terrain; it happens in your body and soul. You feel it. You live it. From an energetic standpoint, when you were in a sexual exchange with another, you were actually woven together into one energetic body, unified in an experience together. This is what I mean when I say an "energetic weave," and it can be true even if the relationship never made it all the way to actual intercourse! In this state of entwined energy, wisdom may be available to you that is beyond traditional knowing. The intuition and empathic connection that allow you to know your partner (even sense their presence before you see them in a room) are a result of this weave of energies. When we understand intimate exchange in this way, it's easy to see how devastating the loss of it can be, no matter the circumstance. The phrase "I feel like I lost a part of myself in that relationship" makes literal sense.

Furthermore, as the energetic weave of sexual union is pulled apart, it can sometimes feel as though by leaving you, betraying you, manipulating you, or abusing you, your past lover has taken something critical from you. You might feel the loss of wholeness in your being, as well as the loss of your self-respect, your trust, or your innocence.

Here's the thing. When intimacies are forged in a state of "not-enough," we surrender our personal power to another through sexual intimacy, thinking that they have something that we lack. In this state, it seems only natural to think that a partner can make us whole and that when they are gone we are even more broken than before. But this idea is flawed at the deepest level. You have never been anything less than whole—except in your mind. Your personal power has never left you; it's only been hidden underneath things like confusion and fear or covered up by the residual energy left there by your past partners. The processes in this book will burn away all that hides this power, and when this type of cleansing is done on this deep energetic level, the mind has no choice but to go along.

Sexual Sovereignty

Recovering your personal power results in a new state of being, one in which you embrace what I call your sexual sovereignty. In simple terms, this refers to a way of being that maintains your independent personal power *even as you foster intimacy with another.* So many women assume that having sexual relationships

always comes with a personal cost—compromise, set-
tling, choosing stability over passion, losing freedom,
getting bored, getting locked into dynamics of power
struggle, and so on. These are seen as the trade-off
for maintaining the overall relationship. But this is
absolutely not the case, and in fact the opposite is
true. These things erode relationships. Recovering
your sexual sovereignty, on the other hand, will fuel
a thriving, heartfelt, easeful, and passionate compan-
ionship that has an indefinite life span.

Only you can foster this relationship with your sexuality. When you do, you will reap enormous benefits:

- ♥ You will reject mean-spirited criticism
  but remain open to generative feedback.

- ♥ You will not compromise your true
  needs, and you will be clear in what you
  can give and accept.

- ♥ You won't settle for less than you
  deserve, and you will be able to express
  your intense gratitude for what you have.

When you cultivate your personal power and
sexual sovereignty, they allow whatever relationships
you have to be shaped by your needs and desires

rather than by ignorance, fantasy, or the desires and needs of the other person only.

In my experience, maintaining your sexual sovereignty is the key to not losing yourself in intimate relationships. It acts as both lighthouse and warning beacon, meaning it guides you to your truth while also sending you intuitive signs whenever you start down a path with another that feels violating to your reclaimed personal power.

Does this mean you'll never feel heartache or be in conflict again? No. Even the best intimate relationships will have challenges from time to time. Reclaiming your power and establishing your sexual sovereignty doesn't mean you'll never face challenges in your intimate dealings with another, nor should it. Change and growth are constant, and the dance of intimacy has many steps. You can and will, however, leave patterns of betrayal, damage, and neglect behind, so that rather than being entangled in dysfunction, you'll be able to gather wisdom and vitality through these challenges.

The chapters ahead are devoted to an exploration of the most significant ways we lose personal power in relationships: neglect, manipulation, and betrayal. Getting into the details of how these play out will prepare you to foster a strong core of personal power and sexual sovereignty and will open the door to the kind of mutually respectful, full-spectrum sexual relationships that are possible for you.

Start with Yourself

Before we go any further together, I'd like to address some things about your past lover or lovers. Let's acknowledge once and for all that people *do* hurt each other, consciously or unconsciously. They *do* diminish and demean each other, intentionally or unintentionally. Your past lover may have fed off of your power and pain, and I'm sure they have plenty of their own issues. But here's the thing: for your recovery to be complete, *none of their issues matter*. As you begin the process of reclaiming your personal power and sexual sovereignty, you must stop trying to analyze or understand who they were, what they were doing, or what you should have said or done in response. Each of these activities in fact keeps you in the grip of a past lover. All you need to know is that this person could not partner with you to your mutual benefit for whatever reason. Even if they seemed hell-bent on destroying something precious to you, it's time to set that aside.

You can only recover your personal power by turning toward yourself. After you understand the basic dynamics, there is nothing to be gained by rehashing your old lover's gifts, flaws, and actions or the complicated story of the relationship. Recovering personal power starts right here, right now—*with you*.

It's time for you to dive deep into your own gifts and choices and to look at how you hold on to the choices of others. Power loss is a convincing illusion. It makes you believe that something crucial to your ability to thrive has been taken from you. Power loss is often married to the authentic grief that comes with the loss of something you treasured or the lost potential of something that you wanted to create. But grieving is its own process, and while it will carve you out and lead you through valleys of despair, it won't steal your power. You can grieve without feeling deflated, diminished, and dimmed. You can mourn the loss of what you loved while at the same time reckoning with the impact of emotional negligence, manipulation, criticism, and betrayal.

You are standing at the threshold of real change. This is your chance to clear away past loverships and create space for deeper intimate connections. The meditation at the end of this chapter will help guide your intention toward retrieving your personal power and reestablishing your sexual sovereignty.

Choosing Your Path

Finally, I want to remind you to view your past relationship or relationships as a sacred initiation, the purpose of which is to serve your evolution in the world. By remaining tied to your past relationships, you are preventing your initiation from coming to fruition; you are stuck in the middle. You can't help but bring the same dynamics into every new relationship you create until you complete the initiation by learning and receiving all that you need from it.

Being caught in the grip of past lovers blocks your ability to know that you are a woman who has a greater capacity for regeneration and recovery than you might imagine. In order to move beyond fixation on the loss, *you must choose this initiation*, even if it wasn't what you wanted.

I'm not implying that you chose this path initially, when you first entered into the relationship. You didn't know it would end like this, or you would never have taken it. This is especially true if you experienced emotional abuse, violence, sexual degradation, or any other brutalities. In order to recover and move forward, you must choose to complete the initiation that began with your past relationship. You have already made that important first step by picking up this book and coming this far.

In the next few chapters, the real work will begin. The good news is that when you complete this initiation, you will be wiser, more loving, and more tapped into your feminine power. When the realities of life bring you challenges in the future, you will find yourself making new choices, staying true to yourself, and not compromising on what is most sacred to you. The self-respect and honesty you claim for yourself through this initiation will carry into your current or future relationships, so that your lover will meet you in ways that you may not have ever experienced.

Action Steps

Meditation is a powerful tool, and integrating a simple, five-minute practice into your daily ritual has a host of wonderful benefits including emotional regulation, pain management, and stress relief. Guided meditations can be particularly helpful when you have time to dive a little deeper and access thoughts and feelings that might not be apparent to you in your busy day-to-day life.

Grounding Through Meditation

We are going to look at the ways in which your personal power is a constant, always present in your body and heart. It cannot be lost or dimmed, only forgotten for a short while.

To begin, find a quiet place where you'll be uninterrupted. This can be outside in nature or somewhere in your home. Sit or lie down comfortably.

Start by taking a couple of deep breaths. Notice any places in your body that are holding tension, and send a little feeling of release to those places. See if they open and expand a bit. Keep breathing.

Next, feel the weight of any part of your body that is touching the floor or the ground— your feet, your legs on a chair, the spread of your back on a bed or the floor. Melt into this weight. As you continue to breathe, imagine that this weight extends beyond your body and reaches down into the earth, like the roots of a massive tree. Feel the energy of your body pushing down and being supported by the earth.

Imagine these roots, deep in the ground, and feel the sensation of drawing nutrients, water, and energy up from the earth and pulling them into your core. Feel your legs, belly, and chest as a strong trunk— supporting your weight and yet soft and flexible, alive with breath.

Next, imagine that from your shoulder blades, radiating up and through your neck, an extension of your spine, are your energetic branches. Drawing on the power of the earth beneath you, funneled through the strong vessel of your body, these branches reach all around you, sensing and feeling the world. Temperature, vibration, weight, sound—all enter your strong core through these branches.

When you are ready, gently open your eyes and return to your physical body. The point of this meditation is to remember—by really feeling it, not just thinking about it—that you have the intrinsic strength of the tallest tree, deeply rooted in the earth and stretching to the skies, available to you at any time. When you rest into the core pillar of strength that always resides within you, nourishment flows into you from all directions. You are connected to sources of support that feed your true vitality and fortify your personal power.

THREE

Healing from Neglect

There is a lighthouse nestled along the rocky central coast of California—a marvel of invention in its day. Inside its tall tower, buffeted by wind and sea spray, sits the lamp, which had to be tended and fueled around the clock. In order to be bright enough to protect ships far out in the ocean, the light from this lamp had to be magnified and reflected in hundreds of bright shining mirrors and lenses, each of which had to be polished and maintained. Without this constant effort, the mirrors and lenses would cloud over with soot, and the light would be dimmed, leaving ships and their crews at the mercy of treacherous waves and rocks. At your best, you are a lamp like this—held up by a strong foundation, a port in the storm lighting the way for yourself and others. And yet you also need regular tending, as neglect of any kind dims your light and clouds your brilliance.

The perils of neglect can be serious, and unfortunately we are starting with an exploration of this topic because it is one of the most common and chronically depleting dynamics women experience in broken loverships. Neglect can play out in many ways, including disregard of your feelings, your value, your time, your needs (both physical and mental), your generosity, and even your very being. On one end of the continuum are thoughtless slights and benign preoccupation; on the other end are disdain and degradation. At its worst, neglect can morph into endless criticism and contempt, which are the death knells of any healthy relationship.

Even after a relationship has ended, the residual impact of neglect from a past lover will leave you feeling dimmed, vacant, or dull. You may be trapped in repetitive thoughts and beliefs that uphold an underlying lack of innate self-worth and disconnection from your radiance. This murkiness can remain even as you shine brightly in other areas of your life, leaving you empty in a way that is hard to explain or understand until you uncover the source of the problem.

If you felt (or feel) dimmed, deflated, or depleted by a previous relationship, it's almost a guarantee that you slipped into the habit of continuing to share your gifts with someone who no longer cherished them as the treasures they are. This can be devastating to your sense of self, even if you were able to maintain self-confidence and self-respect in other ways. I know women, including myself, who have held down full lives that inspired respect and admiration from others and yet have harbored deep-seated sadness and devastating emptiness on the inside.

Interdependence

Our current culture tends to idolize a version of strong female sexuality that is exposed and externally flamboyant. Powerful women are showcased in the media as having bulletproof independence and self-respect that shine no matter what. As appealing as it might be to feel strong and powerful all the time, this isn't realistic in the realm of intimate relationships, where excessive self-reliance more often means being walled off and shut down.

Intimate relationships exist in a *relational field*. You are not singular—that's the whole point. You and your chosen partner deeply influence each other because you are deeply connected. This is not codependence or any other catchphrase for perceived dysfunction in partnership. This is *interdependence*— a natural, inherent aspect of true intimacy. Your chosen lover did (and should) influence your state of being, hopefully toward your greater good and fulfillment. There's nothing wrong with you if you found yourself unable to overcome neglect, indifference, or criticism. Society might tell you to shake it off—that knowing your value will trump anything bad that happens. You can know your value inside and out, but it won't change the fact that if your intimate partner regards you with indifference or contempt, it will dim your radiance.

This is why loneliness from neglect within a relationship feels very different from the occasional loneliness of single life. Within a relationship, you are going to naturally open and turn toward your partner in a dynamic exchange. When that exchange is disparaging, it creates a chronic depletion of energy, which often appears as depression, restlessness, and low self-worth, even if you're otherwise rocking your life.

Residue of Neglect

As we have already explored, intimate relationships are multidimensional, with the energies of you and your partner weaving and flowing through one other. Because of this, you are very vulnerable to the ways in which your partner perceives you. The effect of their disregard can be far more long-lasting than you might expect, as it dims your feminine essence. Even as your understanding grows and you make better choices for yourself, the depletion will linger until you tend to your essence directly and restore your power. You must resolve *never to let anyone neglectful that close to you again.* Neglect in your past is a call to tend your light now, with a greater devotion than you have ever known.

Neglect can manifest in your current state of being in several ways. First, when your partner has failed to recognize the contributions you make, the beauty you shine, the courage you show, or the numerous other ways that you light up their life, you may begin to internalize the *invisibility* that you are receiving from them. For long afterward, you may feel that your contributions are meant to stay in the background.

Second, if you experienced neglect in a past lovership, you will likely find yourself in energetic *neediness*: for attention, reassurance, or even just simple presence from your current or future lovers. This may be present in ways that are out of balance in your current situation and can be harmful to building a new relationship.

Third, neglect can also affect your sense of *worthiness.* The type of worthiness I'm referring to is beyond basics, such as deserving to be respected, heard, safe, and viewed with compassion, though many of us feel a sense of unworthiness in these areas too. When you offer or share the most tender, soulful, sexual aspects of yourself with another, you are opening your vulnerability in a way that is unique to the feminine essence. When you're neglected after sharing your essence, it can leave you with a deep sense of unworthiness that is difficult to understand or explain to anyone who hasn't experienced it.

As you reclaim your personal power and establish your sexual sovereignty, you automatically demand that current and future lovers also show themselves worthy of character and that they prove themselves by their actions in the way they hold you, see you, and care for you, so that you never experience this type of neglect or its aftereffects again. With your power intact, you will move away from those who either refuse or aren't capable of giving you the attention you deserve.

This attention isn't a performance, and it isn't a onetime thing. Surely there will be public climax moments of devotion, such as a marriage ceremony, but what we're really talking about here is day by day, ongoing attention to you and your needs. This quantity time (not just quality time) earns you and your partner the right to receive each other's loving, day after day. If you want your union to thrive, you will choose to attend to each other's needs—again and again, day in and day out.

This doesn't mean that your partner won't have other duties that will pull their attention away from time to time, such as a professional commitment or some unexpected situations that can arise in life. But it's important to realize that even these external circumstances can foster a kind of distance. If this lack of attention continues in the long term, even if it's not due to interpersonal dynamics, the effect on you can be similar. Your heart doesn't make a distinction between the reasons for indifference once it becomes long term. Like any beautiful flower, your feminine essence thrives on regular rhythms of bright light, clear water, and solid ground from which to open into the sky. To thrive, you need the warmth and care of felt love and presence—and any solid partnership must commit to this, even in the chaos of difficult situations. When you don't receive these for any reason, including your own self-neglect, your essence begins to wither.

It's easy to lose sight of the fact that we are animals—creatures of Mother Earth that need certain things to thrive. Nourishing feminine essence can be simple, but it's easy to ignore the need for it. Make a habit of nourishing yourself, and set expectations for your partner to nourish you as well; this will not only help you recover from depletion and past negligence, but also help you get back on track when life circumstances get in the way.

Even as you clarify what you need from others, reclaiming and maintaining your personal power are inside jobs. As you recover from one or more difficult, neglectful past loverships, you might find yourself wishing your former partner would have been different, shown you more attention, honored your feminine essence, etc. This is a moment to bring balance to your thinking about the past. Your former lover couldn't meet you then, and they certainly aren't going to be able to help you now. When you think of the past, let it bring clarity about where you allowed neglect in ways that were harmful to you. After all, your past partner is your teacher and has shown you what is not acceptable. As you reclaim your power, a solid understanding of your past guarantees that your future will be different.

Tending to Your Needs

So how do you begin to restore what has become dimmed or depleted in you over time? First, by turning toward yourself and validating your own needs. This may sound strange, as we are in a cultural moment that prizes self-reliance, and many self-help practices shun anything that might be perceived as codependent or needy. The truth of need has become very misunderstood. We'll dive deeper into this topic in chapter 7, "Reclaiming Your Sacred Needs." For now, I want to be clear that there is nothing wrong with having needs. They are not to be overcome, trivialized, or "healed." In fact, identifying your needs and requesting that they be met are expressions of your reclaimed power and normal parts of a healthy relationship.

As you get more in touch with your feminine essence, you may begin to notice how much our modern world ignores, trivializes, or vilifies your needs as a woman. These include the need for safety, tenderness, honesty, sanctity, honor, reverence, cherishing, creative expression, and loving support for starters. Each individual woman has her own needs, and they will change over time. Whatever they are, your needs are made to be met, not overcome, dismissed, or ignored.

Intertwining with another can be a wonderful, healthy way to get your needs met. Of course, this does not mean that you are entitled to having everything that you think you "need" in any given moment, nor that the world, or your partner, must bow to you. Having needs is simply a normal and necessary part of your essence, and there is nothing wrong with relying on your partner to meet them.

At the same time, as you commit to tending your own heart and your deep reservoir of essential feminine energy, you'll learn how to meet your own needs, especially in moments when your lover is not able or willing to meet you, as well as those times when you are between loverships. This journey of self-love never ends, because your needs will always be changing—pointing the way toward greater fulfillment. Starting here and now, remember this: your needs will be something you bring to relationships as a gift and a confidence, not an apology.

Effortlessness and Nourishment

Before we move on, I want to say a few words about two complementary feminine principles that will serve you in this work: effortlessness and nourishment.

Effortlessness

With effortlessness, you can align your energy with larger forces that are powerful and transformative in and of themselves. Think of any natural cycle—from the waxing and waning of the moon to the four seasons in each year. These don't depend on human effort or intervention, of course. In the same way, there are natural forces at work within you that will allow you to heal and transform with less muscle than you may think you need. For instance, you can align with your own intuition, an awareness of new possibilities, and the healing power of time and distance. Let yourself be served by them rather than trying to force yourself to change. From a practical standpoint, this means you don't need to keep analyzing, talking about, blocking, or generally working hard to "get someone out of you."

Nourishment

Nourishment works hand in hand with effortlessness. As you nourish yourself, your release from the past becomes more effortless. As you well know, when you are depleted, you will hold on to whatever you can in a desperate or confused attempt to meet an authentic need. You are so much more vulnerable when you are depleted. It is often said that we can't *stop* doing anything; we can only *start* doing something else. When you begin a regular practice of nourishing yourself through meditation, self-care, meaningful work, and an enriching and beautiful environment, clearing can become effortless. Your being will naturally release what is no longer serving you.

These principles and practices may seem far too simple to be powerful or to change anything. *It is simple,* and simple truths are often *the most powerful.* One of the deepest truths about the sacred feminine current, which is alive in all women, is that when you turn toward her even a little, she'll magnify whatever you give and return it to you a thousandfold. Think of all the times you've given so much more than you thought you could give, running on fumes with little or nothing in the way of external support or encouragement. There is a natural law at work here, and it has to do with the generosity and generative capacity of the female being. Every time you turn to her, even with a practice this simple, even for fifteen minutes, you are moving mountains.

Action Steps

The practice for this chapter nourishes your feminine essence and restores depleted energy. Again, remember that reclaiming your personal power and sexual sovereignty happens at a level deeper than the mind, so you will need to experience this practice physically in order to nourish your feminine essence. Set aside some time for this—ideally thirty minutes to an hour, but even if you have less than that, just do it. You can shift your relationship to your feminine essence in a single moment of true presence, and you can also return to this exercise to go even deeper.

Recovering Energy Lost from Neglect

To begin, find a place where you can work without interruption, whether outside in nature or somewhere at home that comforts and inspires you. Lie down or sit comfortably. (There is no posture requirement; as long as you are relaxed and undisturbed, those are the key.)

The first step is to meet what has dimmed in you, *resisting any need to try to change it.* That part is very important—and it might be challenging and uncomfortable, since very often when we sense a "problem" our minds immediately go to work trying to "fix" it. Try to head off that response and simply make an authentic connection with the truth of your need by slowing down and really feeling it. You may want to review what you wrote in your journal about your experiences with neglect, as this may help you get more in touch with these feelings.

The goal is to fully meet and claim your feelings around neglect, so that you can release any past lover you are still holding on to. Be willing to be radically honest with yourself about how you actually feel, underneath all the ways you cope, all the ways you shine, all the ways you may feel whole. Let yourself open to the thirst in you, the exhaustion, the sadness, the emptiness, the heaviness. Give these feelings room to just be as they are.

The second step is to explore how the residual impact of a past lover's neglect actually feels inside you. Remember, we are working beyond the level of conscious mind in order to reclaim any dimmed energy, so you want to open your senses. Looking at your energy around neglect, ask yourself: What color is it? What shape is it? What texture is it? Is there a fragrance that comes with it? Are there any images that arise from this?

As you imagine this energy, gently remind yourself to stay with the feeling, rather than starting to tell a story. It can be all too tempting to get sucked into the story of what you should have done or what your past lover should have done, but we're going deeper than that in this process to reclaim your power. After all, your actual power lives here with you now—it never left—but that story is from a long time ago. Do your best to stay with the feelings as they are right now. For instance, you might say, "I feel heavy. It's a metallic, dense and dark, gray boxy kind of heaviness," or "I'm seeing a balloon floating, lost, up in the sky."

Next, try to locate the feeling in your body. Where do you feel heaviness or discomfort? Is it in your heart and chest? In your pelvis? In your eyes or forehead? Bring both hands, one hand on top of the other, to rest and hold awareness on this place. Then just breathe. Focus your energy into your hands and help them bring awareness to this place.

This gesture does three things. First, you are bringing the feeling into the present moment and into your body rather than your mind. Second, you are connecting physical touch to your breath in a way that creates space and movement around this place in you, so that it can begin to shift and change. Third, as you have both hands on your body, centered over the place that is in need, you have also created a closed energetic circuit. Your hands, which are responsible for so much of the energy, care, and creativity that you send out into the world, are now turned fully toward your own body. Through this process you are literally turning the nourishment and attention that you give to the world back to yourself. In this way, you are using your own touch to close the circuit and recharge your inner power.

From this place, allow yourself to open fully to your inner guidance and listen to your needs. What would fill any emptiness, lighten any heaviness, bring beauty and radiance to any place you feel dimmed? This is the time to use your imagination. Really go for it—no limitations, no negotiations! Open up the possibility for desires that are unrealistic, even ravenous. Be open to what arises. Stay with this feeling, and gently dismiss any stories that come up. In this moment, you need not decide what you should *do* next, or what's realistic, or what could or should have happened. This is where you find out what you really want and immerse yourself in your own capacity to tend what is meant to be cherished in you, what is sacred in you. Do this until you feel nourished and a sense of fullness, warmth, or vibration in your body and your hands.

When you feel full and complete, release your hands and just rest in how you feel. Notice the quality of your energy, and review anything else you were shown about yourself and your own internal landscape. At rest here, connected to both your need and the nourishment that meets your need, gently ask your intuitive self if there is a choice or an action you can take in your external life. How can you bring nourishment to yourself?

I invite you to take this time with yourself and to take seriously whatever you receive from the practice, no matter how simple or complex, how rational or completely nonsensical. Stay curious about any clues that presented themselves in this experience. For instance, if you saw the color yellow, perhaps you can buy yourself a dozen yellow roses. If your body felt thirsty or tired, perhaps taking a trip to a stream, lake, or even the ocean would be a good form of self-nourishment. There are infinite possibilities, and they can be everything from simple to extreme. I know someone who did this and as a result dropped everything and went to Thailand, as that is where she always wanted to go and this was nourishing for her. In any case, remember to keep your choices focused on *what would nourish you*. Also remember that what may be nourishing to you right now is doing absolutely nothing. "Doing nothing" is a very potent form of nourishment—especially if your tendency is to take action as a means of avoiding yourself or outrunning your problems.

Watch out for any habit or temptation to turn this experience into a sign or action toward a past lover or another person. This is between you and your essence. Keep it there, because that's where the power to really change everything lies.

Healing from Betrayal and Manipulation

Imagine driving by yourself on a long road trip through the countryside, over gently rolling hills and with clear blue skies overhead, when out of nowhere a dense, silvery fog descends. Suddenly you cannot see even a foot in front of your car. The meteorological term for this phenomenon is a whiteout, and it can be terrifying. In extreme cases, not only is your vision completely obscured, but you can even lose your sense of what is up and what is down. The horizon disappears; there are no shadows, no landmarks, no points of reference.

For those who have experienced the shock of betrayal, it can seem as if your whole life is suddenly enveloped in a whiteout—nothing is familiar, and you've completely lost your bearings. The trust you had in someone has been turned upside down, and while the world still exists, you can no longer see the way ahead.

When betrayal is severe, it can create a level of psychological and emotional shock that can take years to resolve. For this reason, healing from betrayal often requires practices that work to release and ease acute trauma. While you can treat neglect through restorative and nourishing practices, betrayal needs a more active intervention—in much the same way you wouldn't be able to fix a broken bone with chicken soup and rest alone.

The most obvious betrayal is infidelity, which of course can range from a subtle mental connection to a full-blown physical affair, but this is not the only type of betrayal. Betrayals can involve money, dishonesty about something in your partner's past, or lying about present behaviors. Addictions and the behaviors associated with them often leave a sense of betrayal.

Regardless of the specifics, the core of betrayal is that you trusted and believed in the certainty of your circumstances. You relaxed and depended on something or someone, and then the ground was pulled out from under you. New information revealed that reality was very different than what you were led to believe.

When betrayal like this occurs, the first obvious cost to your personal power and sense of self is your ability to trust. This is devastating, both in the moment and in the long term. The effect of betrayal in an intimate relationship will show up in how you trust yourself, how you trust others, and how you trust life as a whole. It can lead to you shutting down, experiencing anxiety, and holding on to deep reservations about opening to intimacy with another. This is often true regardless of how trustworthy your new lover proves to be.

Left unresolved, the residual effects of betrayal can morph into a larger tragedy for you, for your potential partners, and for others in your life as you struggle to trust again. Many times these effects are involuntary, and you might not even be conscious of them—especially if you've been carrying the hurt of betrayal for a long time. For instance, you might find yourself overreacting to harmless situations, instinctively erring on the side of distrust rather than open communication, overcome by jealousy, unable to open your heart and speak clearly, or even unwilling to commit to something new.

Betrayal needs a deep release so that you can bring your side of magic, power, and beauty back to all your relationships. With the shock of betrayal, emotional patterns will continue to play out in the way most traumas do. That is, until you've resolved it fully, you'll interact with the present moment *as if* it were the past trauma, and this will be largely involuntary. Just as with neglect, you can't think your way out of a trauma response; you have to feel it deeply and unwind it on an energetic level, with enough support that you can access the intensity of your feelings without getting lost in them.

Part of our approach to healing from betrayal is informed by my work with trauma release and resolution. We will also focus on the subtler aspects of betrayal that keep you caught up in a past lover and unable to move on. It's time to free yourself, and in this chapter you're going to do just that. As I mentioned, betrayal tends to function as a trauma, so you may have become frozen, anxious, suspicious, or hypervigilant. You may notice yourself checking out, getting confused, or going cold whenever you encounter anything that even hints at vulnerability or sexuality. These signs of a trauma response let you know that your system needs care so that you can return to true well-being and availability to both yourself and your chosen partner.

A World Turned Upside Down

When betrayal is discovered, it is most often accompanied by an awful physical and psychological sense of disorientation. Consider how you have experienced this moment in the past, in your body and heart. Someone you thought you knew one minute became a stranger the next. You might have gotten literally nauseous, dizzy, and faint. The world no longer made sense because you were living in one reality, while your partner was living in another. Furthermore, this person you had trusted in the most intimate way was doing something that was in direct violation of your relationship agreements and your heart's needs. If the deception took place over a long period of time, it may have felt like a tsunami had been building and was now crashing hard as you realized all the moments of dishonesty, lying, and manipulation that went into this betrayal. If you felt like you had been punched in the stomach, you weren't far off.

Seen in this light, it's easy to understand why you would have a lot of psychic catching up to do. The energetic impact of betrayal is so profound that it transcends the psychological and manifests in the physical body. This aspect of betrayal can't be underestimated. While the specifics of the betrayal (the affair, the hidden life, the misuse of funds) can be shocking in and of themselves—and yes, there's plenty to work through and address in the story—underneath that story is the truth that on a foundational level you were living in a reality that wasn't actually real. You were making choices, large and small, in order to craft a life that rested on a foundation without integrity, and now everything is compromised.

You can recover from a betrayal and regain trust, faith, and openness to intimacy again, but in order to begin this process, you must acknowledge the incredible cost to your personal power and sense of self. Here again, the way through a loss like this is to understand and eventually embrace the initiation that is hidden within. There are many insights that can come with a betrayal, but one of the most fundamental is to discover for yourself what is actually true for you and what you can or will build your life upon in the future. While a betrayal will force you to release all that was built upon illusion, it will also leave you naked to the truth of what is not illusion— what will never slip away. This is the strength of who you are. It's your divine feminine essence, which can never be defeated or erased.

Reclaiming Your Power after Betrayal

Betrayal can leave you with two unexpected gifts: first, it can provide a guidebook to your own super-power of intuitive knowing, and second, it can clarify for you which dreams or desires are so important to you that you are willing to pay a high cost for them. This is important, because both your knowing and your dreams need to come with you in order to fully reclaim your personal power and sexual sovereignty.

To begin uncovering these gifts, we will start by consciously recalling everything you lost when you were betrayed. Your list might include the willing-ness to trust, your faith in relationship, your sense of ease, your house, your marriage, your family, your financial well-being, etc. Take a moment to con-sider the full cost of betrayal. List everything in your journal and/or speak it out loud. You might fall into old patterns of shame or victimhood as you do this. While all feelings are valid here, I encourage you to make this list in the spirit of gathering fuel to burn a fire hot enough to complete your initiation into power. Changing your perspective on what hap-pened is part of the recovery process, and you will see that these things are not losses that can never be retrieved; rather, they are sources of fuel. In this way, your past betrayal will become an ongoing source of power rather than a theft of it.

Next, consider any self-betrayal you might have experienced through the gift of hindsight. In other words, look back and consider whether there were ways your intuition was trying to tell you something. If so, what did you do to silence or discount your inner knowing? Please walk a careful line here, as the purpose is self-knowledge, not self-blame. Hindsight is always clearer, and that makes it a resource, not an opportunity to feel ashamed of what you didn't see.

Hindsight gives you a chance to gain greater clarity about how you communicate with the intuitive side of yourself. Once a betrayal has been exposed, you can look back and validate what you missed. For instance, did you get signals from your body, such as a tightening in your gut or heaviness in your heart? Did a thought ever pop into your mind that something was off? Did your intuitive side send you messages through your dreams at night? Were there subtle cues in the body language or behavior of your partner that signaled your intuition? Learning about your internal guidance system is a lifelong study, and as you reclaim your personal power, this type of hindsight inquiry will help you develop more confidence in yourself to trust these intuitive signs in the future.

This leads us to the second unexpected gift of betrayal. In hindsight, you may find ways in which you didn't live up to your own ideals of discernment. You may wonder if you can trust yourself anymore at all. Without self-trust, it will be difficult for you to fall in love again, or to fully enter an intimate relationship when you do fall in love.

As you consider any past betrayal (again looking for knowledge and not blame), can you pinpoint if there was a dream you valued so strongly that you were willing to look away in order to preserve it, ignoring inconsistencies that might have tipped you off sooner? Were there red flags, gut feelings, or perhaps even outright signs that something wasn't right?

This is a fantastic point of inquiry, because it gets to the heart of where you may have betrayed yourself. What are the things for which you were willing to tolerate betrayal? Was it financial security, the dream of a long-term companion, the esteem of your peers, the benefit of your children? Something else? Remember, as you examine this and become brutally honest with yourself as to any motives you had, the point is to harvest power from this experience.

These things were so important to you that you may have compromised yourself on some level to get or maintain them. Rather than judge yourself for that, take a moment and acknowledge how truly important these needs, dreams, or hopes are for you. Hindsight gives you the chance to honor them fully. In the future, you will create a relationship that fulfills these dreams on a foundation of truth and honesty, rather than pretense.

Navigating Through Self-Blame

The next important issue to clear that often arises from a betrayal is self-blame. This is crucial, as internalized self-blame is the surest way for the residual impact of a past lover to continue destroying your power. In my own experience and that of the women I work with, it's amazing how many of us (either subtly or overtly) *blame ourselves* for our partner's hurtful behavior. We may think things like, "If only I had been more loving, more supportive, more sexual, more (fill in the blank)," as if doing any of these things would have prevented the betrayal. It's tempting to want to claim ownership over someone else's choices—it gives a feeling of control in the midst of chaos. But it's simply not true that you're to blame, and thinking that you are drains your energy and keeps you from reclaiming your power. I want to be clear about something right now: regardless of any ways in which you need to grow, choosing to betray you was a choice *your partner made*. It's not a reflection of you at all. It's a reflection of them.

You often hear in spiritual and self-help circles that "there are no victims." In my view this is an unhelpful characterization when it comes to betrayal, because it's just a fact that sometimes, in some circumstances, we are on the receiving end of some really nasty stuff. Almost all of us, at some point in our lives, will be deceived, manipulated, betrayed, or overpowered. In these situations, we are victims. We gain power not by denying victimhood, but by making choices after the experience that reclaim our power and wholeness. In other words, how will we choose to respond to the situation? Will we gain wisdom? Will we heal? Will we love ourselves even more, as we are doing right this moment? Will we learn to make different choices in the future?

One of the most insidious dynamics of power loss is to believe that you are responsible for putting yourself in a victim role. When someone dominates you, lies to you, overpowers you, or somehow makes you small—that is *their choice*. At the end of the day, this is someone who is incapable of honoring you—*not because you don't deserve it,* but because they have not yet grown into their own capacity for honor. Don't take it on. You are enough.

Transforming Shame

Finally, very much related to self-blame are the feelings of shame and humiliation that come with a betrayal. When we realize what has been going on, we feel naive and stupid, and if infidelity was a part of the betrayal, we almost always compare ourselves to "the other woman" and feel less-than. We are ashamed as word travels through our circle of friends and community and it becomes everyone's business. Shame turns everything into an accusation that there is something wrong with you, your choices, your history, and your life. It can sap your joy and drain your energy.

The antidote to shame is radical, unconditional reverence. A step beyond self-respect, reverence implies that not only are you going to treat yourself with respect, but you are actually going to treat yourself like the sacred vessel you truly are. Treating yourself as sacred might seem foreign, maybe even presumptuous. But it's essential to reclaiming your power and restoring balance to your life—especially if you've experienced private and/or public humiliation. Make three things your priority: (1) protect your vulnerabilities (steer clear of triggering people or situations); (2) have faith in your capacity to heal; and (3) care for yourself with tenderness. Put simply, do only what brings you comfort or clarity. Shame will bring neither of these, so there is no place for it.

Lastly, shame and self-blame are signals that let you know it's time to nourish your heart and soul. They can offer a path to a certain level of self-mastery and an initiation into ferocious self-love and self-care. When I say self-mastery, I mean the ability to make moment-by-moment choices that direct your attention only toward what nourishes you. And by ferocious self-love, I mean stoking the fires of your well-being and personal power, turning all your passion away from previous relationships. Ferocity plus mastery will protect you and light your way on a new path.

Manipulation

Another aspect of past sexual relationships that can leave a devastating impact—and often goes hand in hand with betrayal—is manipulation. This is a devastating form of control and a way to maintain power, and it can plant seeds that will continue to grow in your psyche long after you've physically left the relationship. Manipulation can make you feel broken, confused about your boundaries, or inherently flawed. It essentially fractures your confidence and personal power.

Another important thing to know about manipulation is that it is also a form of betrayal in the relationship. In other words, when you first met your past lover, he or she probably didn't introduce themselves as a manipulator. Because manipulation often happens slowly and progresses over time, you likely didn't realize the betrayal until you finally woke up.

When you do snap out of the spell of deep dysfunction and emotional manipulation, you might again feel an intense shame about having allowed yourself to be so fooled, so controlled, for so long. Looking deeper, you may find that your manipulator used shame as a tool to control you. For instance, were you made to feel ashamed about your needs? Or your "flaws"? Or your "misperceptions" about things? Manipulators often use your own insecurities against you, making you believe that you are the problem in the relationship and dumping responsibility for their disturbed actions on you.

In this way, the shame that you are feeling now has its roots in the shame they wrapped you in while you were still in the relationship. It is part of the residual effect. Know this: *there is NO SHAME in losing yourself in the manipulation of another.* Truly, some people are disturbingly gifted at the art of manipulation. They're masterful. They thrive on controlling people that have an emotional, sexual, or financial bond to them. When you wake up out of a power dynamic that is as entrenched as these often are, you might continue to feel shame about it all simply because you are so used to feeling fundamentally ashamed about who you are.

Manipulators thrive on keeping you from your power. This sense that you weren't powerful enough, more powerful than they were, can persist long after the relationship ends. The first step to breaking out of the residual shame is realizing you have nothing to be ashamed of and that in fact your greatest power comes in the form of your honesty, your vulnerability, and your ability to set boundaries.

Action Steps

The following exercises can help you cultivate clarity and discernment regarding your perception of yourself and your past loverships.

Getting Clear on What's True and What's Not

If you went through this long enough, your own self-perception may be skewed by your partner's perception of you. They may have told you things about yourself for long enough that they have left impressions in your psyche. It is important to name these impressions and the dynamics that kept them in place and then separate them from what is really true for you.

Let's do an exploration. To start, create two columns in your journal. In the left-hand column, list words you think your partner would use to describe you—your personality, your appearance, your strengths and your weaknesses. In the right-hand column, list how each of these words makes you feel. Try not to think too much about whether your partner really thought this way about you, as ultimately it's not important (we can't ever know for sure what someone else is thinking). Our goal here is to get a more complete picture of the impressions that were left inside you—what you're dealing with right now.

As you reconnect with the past in a more conscious way, I want to warn you again about the dangers of getting caught up in the definition of your former partner and who they might be. It can be an energetic trap. The purpose is not to relive these experiences in your mind and feel the emotions all over again, but rather to study the past experience and see it for what it was so that you can *step outside of it*. Often when it's on paper, you can spot the insanity and unreality of what your partner encouraged you to believe about yourself that just isn't true. Really seeing this, and believing it, is a huge step in reclaiming your personal power.

When you have completed your list, take a moment to consider what ritual might help you heal from the impressions left on your being. You could burn the list or shred it and release it to the wind. Alternatively, you could keep it in a special place as a reminder of what never to believe about yourself again. In any case, the point is to seal this up in a ritual way and give it an end point, to bring yourself fully and gently into your present moment.

Identifying Fantasy vs. Reality

When betrayal occurs, we can often hold on to a fantasy version of our past lover, even after the betrayal is exposed. The same goes for coming to terms with manipulation, as we realize that the stories that allowed us to continue in the relationship are no longer true for us and yet we may still hold on to them in some way. So many of us replay a fantasy version of our past lover that isn't reality. Creating the following two lists can help you see the past more clearly, as well as show you what's truly important to you in a relationship going forward.

First, create a list about your past lover where you describe your vision of them as a fantasy. This outlines what you thought they were, what you held out hope that they would become, or what they may have fooled you into believing about them. Here's an example:

Fantasy

1. He was so good with the kids.

2. He was so present and connected.

3. He was such a good provider.

4. He was such an amazing lover.

5. We had a magical soul connection.

6. He was savvy and sophisticated.

Next, make a list of what actually happened, who this person actually was. Don't qualify it by trying to hold on to their good qualities or some sense of the value of the relationship. In this list, focus on the areas where the betrayal or manipulation occurred. Here's an example:

Reality

1. When he traveled for work, he would pick up women at bars.

2. He was an amazing lover for the first three months but then lost interest and started watching porn instead of making love to me.

3. He spent money on himself rather than on us.

4. He never washed his own dishes or offered to help with any of the household expenses, letting me do it all without even a thank-you.

5. He criticized the way I dressed and made comments about my "extra ten pounds," making me feel awkward and self-conscious.

Get real about the way this person *actually treated you*. What actions shaped your relationship, beyond words and sentiments?

Perhaps at the start of the relationship it was wonderful. Quite possibly it will take some time to fully reckon with the person they became or revealed themselves to be.

I'm not referring to self-responsibility and mature inquiry into what role you played in perhaps undermining trust or intimacy. This exercise centers on your impressions of your partner, and again I encourage you to set aside self-blame as you work through it. This doesn't mean pretend that you didn't play a part—because in fact taking responsibility for yourself and your actions is a huge part of the process of breaking free from past lovers. We will devote the next chapter to it. Internalizing blame is different than taking responsibility, and as you work with these concepts, you will get better and better at knowing the difference.

Inquiry Practice

This next practice will mine your experiences of betrayal and manipulation from past relationships and transform them into wisdom.

First, make four columns in your journal: The Truth, How I Knew, Why I Allowed, and The Gold.

The Truth: In the first column, describe truthfully what happened in your past relationship. Now that you're outside of it and have the power of hindsight, you can characterize the main points and qualities. For example:

- ♥ He was having an affair with Natalie.

- ♥ He was shaming me to conceal his own insecurities.

- ♥ He was interested in the financial security I was providing, but not in me.

How I Knew: In the second column, describe how you knew things were off and what signs were available to you. For most women I work with, they knew in some way but didn't want to believe it. Whether it's our own unwillingness to see or the masterful manipulation of our partner, when we look back we can see the body language, signs, situations, and explanations from our partners that defied common sense. Look deeply at how you knew then or how you might have known if you were willing to admit it. Here lies your power for the future: getting in touch with you intuition to uncover things as they are.

Why I Allowed: Next, think about why you allowed this behavior. With gentleness and open honesty, look into why you allowed what was, in the end, unacceptable and damaging to you. Security, a sense of caretaking, a desperate need to be loved and seen by this person, a longtime fantasy of the perfect relationship, shame, not wanting to have a public divorce . . . it could be any number of things. Be as specific as you can, because this is how you unhook yourself *from the inside* from the dynamics of the past. This is how you free yourself now and have enough awareness of your motives to stop creating these dynamics in the future.

The Gold: In the fourth column, you get to claim the gold—the hidden treasure in your experience. What do you have now that you otherwise would never have attained? What commitment to yourself have you made that you will never betray? What did this experience initiate you into as a woman of power, wholeness, and clarity of mind?

This practice is powerful because it moves you forward with a sense of purpose for the path ahead. It can be tempting to linger in the dramatic story of it all or numb out because it feels too painful. Either of these options can leave you confused about why you're still feeling stuck. Whenever you find yourself questioning yourself, your choices, your worth, or your future, you can do this exercise to get some perspective. It can help you name whatever subtle residual impact might be jamming up your works. It is also a great inquiry to do when you find yourself hung up on the past, feeling depleted by the loss of a relationship, or intimidated by moving forward. Connecting to the pain and loss allows you to go mining for the gold that has been forged by your experience.

You have everything you need inside yourself. You are now and forever your own deepest ally and advocate, and you will continue to be so in every intimacy you choose from here on out. Take the time to reckon with betrayal, manipulation, and mistreatment and receive their gifts of strengthening your intuition and learning what's important to you. Free yourself from self-blame and shame, and you are taking another step toward reclaiming your personal power, establishing sexual sovereignty, and becoming an ally to yourself that you can fully trust, with the certainty that you will never abandon yourself again.

FIVE

Taking Responsibility for Your Own Behavior

The first warm day of spring can feel like a revelation, especially for those who live in a colder climate. Spring invites you to throw open your windows for some fresh air and light, and you may feel the urge to tackle deep cleaning and larger organizing projects that have been sitting through the winter.

This chapter is an invitation to experience your own energetic spring-cleaning, as up until this point, we've explored past relationships from the perspective of what your partner "did wrong" in the relationship. Of course, the other important factor at work here is your own words and actions in past loverships, as these also contribute to a strong and lasting grip on you. This is an opportunity to face the mess that we collect and hold on to—to take inventory of ourselves. When we engage in this kind of gentle ownership of our behaviors, we can accept our whole selves and put underlying expectations and emotions in their proper places with care. With the windows open, we can move forward with even greater clarity. To do so, we will look at the kinds of things you said or did, or things you neglected to do, and learn how to own these and put them to work on your journey of healing and wholeness.

No relationship dynamic is ever one-sided. For every time you have felt neglected, there may well be a time you were neglectful. Power struggles, manipulation, criticism, withdrawal of attention—each of these is often a two-way street. When you look at your part in past relationship woes, you may feel regret. Regret is a powerful teacher, and you can harness it in a constructive way to keep you aware and help you grow—so long as you know how to work with it.

Regrets leave a certain amount of bound-up energy in you—they can pull at your attention, waiting to be seen, understood, loved, and accepted. Regrets can also come with a sense of loss, grief, sadness, or longing. Our exploration into regret will help you reckon with the choices you made and liberate any energy that may still be bound up by those choices.

When you feel wronged in a relationship, it's easy to focus on the flaws or the lack of integrity in your former partner. Sometimes you will focus solely on the behaviors that are most evident, like an infidelity, but this can prevent you from important self-reflection about your own lack of integrity, even if it played out in small ways. If you want to be fully free and to move into healthy intimacies from this point forward, it is absolutely necessary that you get very honest with yourself about how you contributed to the disintegration of love and trust in your relationship. In other words, you can't really get anywhere until you are willing to own your part.

Once again, it's important to remember that this process is about self-reflection and not self-abuse. This might be the trickiest moment we've encountered so far—since looking at your own actions of course fires up your inner critic. It will help to remember that your purpose here is to learn from any regrets you have and to use them as fuel to learn more about yourself, develop your integrity, and ultimately reclaim your personal power and sexual sovereignty. You must walk a fine line here between taking on too much responsibility and refusing to acknowledge the part you played. Yes, you did things you now regret; you acted in ways that compromised your integrity and that hurt your partner and the relationship. But despite anything you did, you are not the cause of the hurtful or even cruel behavior of your partner, nor are you responsible for it.

How will you know when you are veering too far in one direction or the other? Pay attention to your feelings—they will be your guide. If you feel ashamed, guilty, or broken, look at that as a sign that you are taking on too much personal responsibility for the mistakes of the past. This is not to say that there isn't truth underneath these feelings, but the fog of shame or guilt will only cloud your perception. These feelings are a sign that you are beating yourself up, and you'll have to be both honest and gentle as you dig deep.

As you're appraising your past behaviors, remember that the point of this is to move *away* from misperceptions about your lack of worth and *toward* the full expression of all that you are. Shame and fear slow this process. Keep your intentions on reclaiming your personal power and know that it's okay to discard whatever doesn't serve your true nature.

Let's take a look at some common behavior patterns that can subtly feed neglect, power dynamics, and lack of trust in a relationship. Your specific regrets may differ somewhat, but chances are you'll see yourself in least one of these. We're looking at the actions and mind-sets that keep you from living out your deepest values. In working with many women over the years, and in my own experience, I have found that there are some ways in which we push away the very thing we are most yearning for through these behaviors.

Expectations and Entitlement

The first behavior pattern to examine in your past is a sense of entitlement—any ways in which you acted or felt like you were owed something. It's important to keep perspective here, because of course you are deserving of good things. Entitlement embodies a sense of superiority and ungratefulness, and it creates expectations of your partner—or of life itself—that can never be met. This kind of expectation engenders a never-ending game of not-enough, as each time your partner reaches the goalpost, you move it a little farther away. In this way, entitlement is a way of punishing or undermining your partner, often striking at the heart of the tender places inside them. The negative energy of expectation and entitlement pushes away the good things you wanted in the first place.

When it comes to relationships, entitlement thrives on the desire for control, as we demand what we think we deserve and we want it in a certain way. Control shuts down our admiration, our curiosity, and our ability to be in the moment—and these are the great joys of being in partnership! When we demand that our partners show their love through specific actions, by saying specific things, or by just knowing what we really want without us having to tell them, we sap joy from our partnership. We shut down our partner's desire and ability show their love for us in their own way.

It is a gift for someone to meet your needs, not an obligation. Your part of the deal is to receive your partner's genuine attempts to meet your needs, to love you—even if it doesn't always fit your imagined perception of how it "should" be done. You can't do that if you're pulling, pushing, and demanding. A relationship is a dance, not a forced march.

Criticism

Criticizing your partner is a surefire way to destroy trust and set the stage for a breakdown in appreciation, communication, and intimacy. Criticism is tied to entitlement and expectation, because it's how you tell your partner all the ways in which they are failing to reach your standards. You may think that your critiques are in fact valuable and helpful advice. But the truth is that you don't have to criticize someone in order to inspire growth—and really, criticism usually shuts down growth and change, because when people feel attacked they tend to get defensive and stubborn.

Love thrives on acknowledgment, honor, and free choice. Love moves into the world through thoughts, words, and actions, and how you express yourself reflects your sense of self-respect and self-knowledge. Have you ever criticized a partner, only to realize that there's a deeper misunderstanding or unresolved frustration going on with you that has very little to do with them?

Anger and Bitterness

Anger and bitterness are usually the result of a lack of personal nourishment and broken boundaries. These patterns can also emerge as a response to unresolved injustices, heartbreak, or broken dreams from the past. If you came to your relationship already bitter, jaded, and looking for inevitable character flaws in your partner, then you probably had a hand in creating, or at least magnifying, those flaws.

Only one person in the world can turn the bitterness of your life into medicine. That person, of course, is you. If you can look back and see how your bitterness, coldness, or anger made a past relationship a hard, unforgiving road rather than a garden fertile with promise, then please—take a pause, take a breath, and make the promise to yourself that you will tend your own garden. Only you can bring your heart back to life and mend what feels broken before you expect anyone to meet you there.

After all, you will invite any future lover into your garden—into the sweetness that lives and grows in you. Even more importantly, the garden is where *you* live—what fills you and defines you. If bitterness colored any of your past relationships, be honest, be brave, and revere your dreams enough to bring yourself back into vibrant, flowering life.

Sexual Manipulation

Sexual manipulation is just what it sounds like, and it occurs anytime you use your sexual energy to manipulate, control, or influence your partner. When you reflect on the relationship, can you see any ways in which you offered sex as a reward to get what you wanted? Were there times that you withheld sex as punishment in an attempt to control certain behaviors? If so, know that this didn't serve your partner, and it certainly didn't serve you. Looking back now, you have the opportunity to free yourself of this pattern, which is a long-standing and deep-seated habit of several of the women I work with.

Many of us grew up with cultural norms that reinforced the notion of female sexuality as something we can use to get what we want. Breaking the pattern of sexual manipulation opens the door to truly reciprocal, sustained intimacy.

If you have used sexuality to manipulate, even subtly, you have been complicit in whatever larger patterns of manipulation may have played out between you and a past partner. Not only were you seducing your partner into things that weren't authentic for them, but you were acting in ways that weren't authentic to you. As you develop sexual sovereignty, you will own the fact that pleasure must be freely given and gratefully received, never used to manipulate someone else.

Sometimes a sexual bond is all that holds an otherwise dysfunctional relationship together. Sometimes withholding sexuality drives infidelity and betrayal. If you participated in sexual manipulation or control, notice if it brought you anything that you valued or loved. I would guess it did not.

Dishonesty

There are many reasons why you may have chosen to be dishonest in your past relationship. Perhaps you hid details because you were ashamed of your actions and fearful of the consequences, or maybe your goal was to keep a part of yourself outside of the relationship. You may have even felt the relationship would end if your lover knew "that" about you or your past. While these reasons may sound worthy of deceit, each of them brings only short-term security and all but ensures a serious breach of integrity and a blow to your connection.

Relationships built without a solid foundation of honesty will wobble in all sorts of ways. True intimacy requires courage, and it requires both partners to stand firm in vulnerability and transparency and see what emerges.

You might have felt you had to hide something because your partner couldn't or wouldn't be able to hear you and understand. Maybe your partner didn't make a safe space for that kind of vulnerability. By moving forward without honesty, you were only boxing yourself into a relationship that couldn't hold you. Even worse, by depriving your partner of the truth, you ensured you would never know whether or not they could show up for you or wanted to know you more deeply. We often withhold information or hide parts of ourselves in a desperate attempt to control the outcome of the relationship, to keep the relationship together, or to protect ourselves in other ways.

Take the time now to feel the true costs of dishonesty. How did it affect the growth potential of your love? Think of this: a relationship based on convenient white lies (or big lies) can last forever and never become real, while an honest relationship can last only a night and still be one of the most authentic expressions of your life.

The Power of Moving Past Regret

I encourage you to put your regrets to work as fuel for the burgeoning integrity in you. As you work through your own regrets, you will set yourself free by claiming and coming to peace with your actions, thereby gathering the wisdom to move forward and build any potential new partnerships as your best self.

In the end, the process of clearing past lovers begins and ends with *you*. Control, manipulation, and withholding might feel like power moves in the moment, but I would argue that these habits actually point to a profound lack of feminine power. An empowered woman is fierce and gentle, strong and vulnerable. You are all this and more. I am sure of it. So claim your regrets and own your future.

Action Steps

The ritual and exercises that follow are designed to help you accept and let go of your regrets so you can continue forward into authentic, empowered intimacy.

Connecting with Regret

Allowing yourself to explore the fullness of your regrets will also help you forge a greater, more authentic version of yourself. True regret or remorse, even embarrassment, about the ways in which you have chosen to behave in the past can be a powerful teacher as you refine yourself into someone you really respect and who is truly available for cultivating a trustworthy intimacy.

Set aside some time in a quiet place, and center yourself with a few deep breaths. You may want to light a candle with the gentle intention of fueling your growth. Bring to mind one of the lingering regrets you have about your behavior in a past relationship—it can be any of the modes described in this chapter or something else entirely.

Now, envision "past you"—that is, the person you were when you behaved in this way. Really see her, sitting in front of you. Look deeply into her eyes. See if you can feel the deep need behind the actions you now regret. Do you sense an ache of loneliness? A fear of loss? Maybe you see that her eyes are clouded with self-obsession. As you gaze at her, bring your hands to your heart, and call up the cycle of warmth you found there in the last chapter. Extend some of this warmth past you, imagining a burst of warm, loving energy traveling from your heart to hers.

Take as long as you need in this place, flowing love to your past self—just as she was then. Finally, as you wrap up, you can say a few words out loud or in your head to her. You might say, "I see that you gave the best you knew. Now I know so much more. I forgive you," or "I'm grateful that we will grow together by facing this difficult thing."

When you are ready, gently open your eyes and return to your physical body. While this former self is in a way always a part of you, you have also released her hold on you and her impact on your future actions. You know more now than she knew then.

Exploring Intimacy and Your True Desires

This exercise works with any regrets you have around sexual manipulation. In your journal, list as many times as you can think of that you used sexual intimacy, or withheld it, in order to get something you wanted or to gain the upper hand.

Next to each item on your list, write down what it is that you hoped to achieve or shut out through your actions. Here are some examples:

Withholding sex: Wanting to be acknowledged for everything I was doing

Pretending to be excited: Thinking there was something wrong with me

Faking an orgasm: Wanting to get it over with without having to submit fully to the experience

Finally, give yourself some new affirmations based on your list that will guide you in a relationship that serves the freedom and sexual vibrancy in you, no manipulation necessary. For example:

♥ I will share my need to be seen and appreciated outside the bedroom, so that resentment doesn't cloud my desire to be intimate.

💜 I know I am whole, and I accept and honor the beautiful ebb and flow of my sexual desire.

💜 As I find safety in my partner's arms, I commit to staying present, authentic, and vulnerable so that I can celebrate our intimacy with joy.

This week, practice repeating these affirmations each morning. Notice how speaking these intentions helps you set the tone for the rest of the day. I encourage you to make new affirmations as your wants and needs change over time and to continue this practice indefinitely.

Making Amends

You may find in this exploration that it feels appropriate to make amends to a former partner. You may want to write a letter, call, or meet in person to express sincere apologies for your own part of disrespect, betrayal, or negligence.

Through this whole process we are aiming to reclaim self-respect and self-knowing. If you acted in ways that you don't respect, making amends may be an effective way to access self-forgiveness and restore integrity, but please be cautious about getting yourself further entangled. The only value of your regrets is that they will point you toward where you are heading now, what you are becoming now. If making amends feels like it's an important part of that, great, but it's by no means necessary to include your former partner in this process at all. This is ultimately in you, for you.

SIX

Soaking Up the Positive

Up until now, we've been working with relationships or experiences within relationships that have been negative, self-depleting, or otherwise unhealthy in some way. These relationships hold a certain type of growth potential based on learning from the discomfort they created.

In this chapter, we are going to turn our attention to the positive experiences we've had within even our most problematic loverships. Women describe these to me as, "That lover gave me the most mind-altering, ecstatic sex I've ever had," or "We experienced a profound intimacy, a deep love that touched my core being." Since these experiences weren't negative, sometimes the women I work with wonder why we need to cover them at all. But in order for you to be fully available to yourself and to your current or future lovers, it's important to break free of *all* your past experiences—the amazing ones and the negative ones alike. After all, the past is still the past, and clinging to it can keep you from opening to your current or future lover fully.

While we've been focused on breaking the grip of past experience, in this case it's more accurate to think of fully absorbing these positive experiences. Their hold on you might take the form of comparison, nostalgia, or just not being able to recover from the magnetic pull of an experience that touched you deeply. You can gain personal power and sexual sovereignty here too, if you adjust your thinking and your energy in regard to this experience.

You most likely don't want to lose the gift—the beauty and magic—of what you experienced, nor should you. If it touched your heart and soul, there was truth in it, even if it got tangled up in later complications and heartbreak. An amazing experience can linger, preoccupy you, or keep you bound up in fantasy only when you haven't understood your part in it yet. Until you do, you will be held by the grip of this past lover, thinking it was all about them.

In other words, we remain bound by our amazing experiences because we haven't owned the extent to which they were ours—we felt them in our bodies, our minds, and our hearts. We give all the credit to a great lover, not owning our part in making it magical. Once we realize this, we can unleash any untapped power that's bound up in the residual impact of positive experiences. For instance, here are a few common myths we may tell ourselves about these relationships, along with the corresponding truth statements:

> MYTH: That lover was amazing and took me to places I've never been before! How will I ever get there again? There's no one quite like him/her out there anywhere.

> TRUTH: I am so grateful to have opened in that way. My body is different now. My experience of sexuality is expanded now. What I felt in my body (the love, the orgasm, the opening, the magic) is now a gift that is mine forever, to cultivate within myself and to share with whomever I choose, when I am gifted with a situation that I discern to be honoring and right for me.

MYTH: Soul mates are meant to be forever. I must have failed somehow.

TRUTH: Soul mate relationships have their own timing and deep wisdom. They can come to be a lifelong relationship or a short-term catalyst toward growth. I touched something soulful in that relationship, and it was a gift, but then things changed. The best thing I can do with the beauty of that experience is to honor it and release it. I can choose to surrender with grace.

MYTH: So many men touched my heart and soul, fell in love with me, and then just walked away. There must be something lacking in me or secretly wrong with me.

TRUTH: Many men are actually intimidated by the potency of female sexuality and often run away or sabotage the relationship because the energy is so big and so strong. It's not that I am lacking anything—it's that it requires courage and emotional resiliency on both sides to sustain a powerful love/sex relationship.

MYTH: If a love like that can fail, then any love will.

TRUTH: Love, sexuality, and I are ever evolving. It is a mystery and a grace when love sparks and then finds the strength to build and stay true over time. Love is always beyond imagining—and rarely foreseen. Just because I can't see it yet doesn't mean I have any idea what the mystery has in store for me.

MYTH: The passion we experienced was instantaneous and extraordinary. It swept me up and away and was the most right I've ever felt with anyone. How can any relationship even touch that?

TRUTH: There is passion that ignites immediately and passion that burns slow but hotter and deeper over time. Many times the epic connections that start hot and huge do not have the foundation to support such fire over time, and they fall apart. No relationship will ever bring quite the same beauty and heat, but a flame that builds over time will actually last, and as it lasts, it will take me deeper and further than I could possibly have gone in that relationship that fired so fast and hot, but lacked solid ground and emotional stability.

The fact is that when you have a truly beautiful, life-changing sexual or emotional experience with someone else, there is no doubt that it has very much to do with them, but it never could have been without you. You get to own these experiences as a part of your own personal power and sexual sovereignty.

In my case, some of my past loverships have been downright overwhelming in their beauty, leaving me destitute when they ended. Yet the despair that can come from losing a deep intimacy with another pales in comparison to living a life of estrangement from myself—disconnected from my personal power and sexual sovereignty. That is far more painful.

For this reason, I have come to see my amazing past connections as lifesaving, rather than heartbreaking. None of these lovers were meant to be my king, to be my companion all the way through the long walk of life. They came forward from my soul's longing to know *herself,* and they showed me what I am capable of experiencing. In that, they served a very sacred role on my path. They were like an initiation—which as you know can be harrowing and rigorous. So I invite you, as the heroine of your own story, to look back and ask yourself: What did this relationship come to teach me? What did I learn about myself? What will I take with me from this experience? What will I become as I integrate the depth of the experience into the fullness of my personal power and sexual sovereignty?

Grieve, Absorb, and Claim

In order to release the hold that past positive experiences may have on you, I invite you to see them as part of your full feminine range, remembering that they could not have happened without you. In order to make the most of them on your journey, you must process them by grieving their loss, soaking in the positive, and claiming your part. Only then can you set yourself free.

Grieve

When these peak experiences get lost or complicated by other, more difficult, relationship dynamics, you might feel a unique kind of grief. You might feel dulled and empty or have a sense of anguish and longing for an experience you think you will never have again.

But is that really true? In my view, this is actually a convincing illusion. Yes, on one level the experiences you have had through intimacy with another will be unlike any other, and these were related to the magic of your partner—but at the same time, these experiences belong to you. Feel your grief, and use the following exercises to absorb the positive, claim what will nourish you, and release it forever.

Absorb

Some past loverships are big, multidimensional, even life-changing. Your participation in a union at that depth leaves an undeniable impact on you. If you still long for it, even when it's clear that it's over, then you can be sure that you haven't yet absorbed all that was given to you in this intimate experience. Being bound up in past experience of any kind—negative, positive, or a mix—prevents you from attainting full presence in the now.

The important thing for you to know is that the great expanse you felt with this other person is *still your expanse.* The images, feelings, and energy are still yours, and you can choose to absorb them deeply. Even though the relationship or encounter is over, the power of transformation that was offered to you through this experience need not be diluted and dissipated. It is still there for you, no matter what.

With this in mind, I invite you to inquire more deeply by writing responses to the following questions in your journal.

- ♥ What was epic about your experience?

- ♥ How did you feel in your body? How was your heart awakened and connected? In what ways did the relationship fulfill your longing and your passion?

- ♥ What still captures your attention today?

- ♥ As you reflect on this experience, can you become more aware of how you created it through your own beauty and specialness—your own soul?

- ♥ What quality of life, what promise, came into your life through this person, this intimacy?

Claim

The next and most important step is that you must claim the feelings that were ignited in you, along with any wisdom you received as a result of the intimate exchange between you and this other being. Often when you're in a state of longing for a past partner, your attention is caught by them—how they felt, how they smelled, how they spoke to you or touched you, how they showed up in ways that fulfilled you. You may also be caught up in what you were together—the passion, the lovemaking, the dreams shared, the heightened energy of your togetherness.

However, in order to claim this experience for yourself fully, you must go one step further and bring your focus home, to yourself. The experience with them is over; they have moved on and are not a part of your present life. But the ripples of the experience are still moving through you. You are still here, and you're not going anywhere.

Whatever aliveness and passion rose up in you during a past lovership came from you. One way to remember this is to think of your past partner as a clear mirror, rather than the passion or the aliveness itself. They only reflected the deep pools within you—your passion. Now that you're aware of it, you can integrate this passion and vitality into your every choice, even small ones, and rebuild the sense of pleasure and wholeness that comes from within. Claim the gift you were given. It was always meant for you, and it was always meant to wake you up.

In my experience, I have come to regard each of my lovers as a chariot, on which my one true Love rides to meet me. When I say Love with a capital L, I mean the universal Love that flows everywhere all the time. I adore it, and it adores me, and I know that Love will continue to arrive for all of us in whatever form it can so that we can meet and share this gift. Using your own language, I invite you to see the forces of Love that want to open you, please you, cherish you, and meet you in soul as well as body. When things end with what felt like a divine soul mate or deeply meaningful, rare sexual intimacy, your communion with this greater Love will bring you immense comfort.

Making Ritual Yours

At the end of this chapter, I have included a few rituals. The power of any ritual is only as strong as the experience is meaningful for you personally. The rituals here, and any of the others in this book, can and should be adapted to your needs and desires. There's no right or wrong here—just what moves you. Keep it authentic, simple, and real to you. You may want to invite a close friend to witness and hold space with you, or you may prefer to do it alone if that feels more comfortable. Use your voice and speak out loud, or rest in the power of silent prayer—or some combination of the two. Remember that breath, physical action, and time are all powerful factors in ritual. Set your imagination free.

Whether you are lingering over an experience that was simply beautiful or you're caught up in the confusion of having a relationship that was equal parts wondrous and damaging, only through the process of honoring, absorbing, and putting to rest the lost beauty can you move fully into your present moment and any relationships that are now opening for you.

Remember, all beauty is for your nourishment, even if it must be released and returned to the earth to grow a different kind of garden than you expected. Let yourself become awakened by the gifts of intimacy, rather than devastated by the loss of it. You are far more than you can imagine, and what you may have touched with a lover is just the beginning of the pleasure that is your birthright as a woman.

Action Steps

Following are three rituals that will help you claim the positive from past relationships and release any residual hold they have on you. I invite you to take an hour or so somewhere quiet, nurturing, and beautiful and commit to exploring them.

Absorbing Moments of Connection Ritual

Through this ritual, you will locate the remembered physical experience of being with your former lover and let it come alive as something you can access in the here and now. This process lays down the path to sexual sovereignty. After all, partners can serve as catalysts—but they can only awaken something that *already lives within you.* You can learn to nourish this feeling regardless of circumstance, with or without future partners.

Your sexual energy is your own. What you touched in an amazing intimacy is *what you are capable of touching.* The heights of pleasure or depth of connection you found are your heights, your depths. Of course, stoking the passion within yourself and cultivating it as your life force will always be a different landscape than the charged relational field of lovership. But lovers come and go, ebb and flow. You are what remains—beautiful, constant, and complete.

To begin, find a quiet, nurturing place and get settled in. Scan back through the experience you shared with your partner, keeping your focus on the aliveness that came forward in you. As you revisit moments of pleasure and connection, explore the magic in you, the way you felt.

What came alive? Give it a color, a fragrance, a texture, and recall the sensations in your body. Perhaps your heart was warm and open and you could feel the aliveness overflowing into your breasts, your nipples, like golden honey. Perhaps your whole body felt softer and more translucent, as if light were streaming out of you, glowing and radiant. Perhaps you felt a deep vibration in your body, your belly, or your sexual centers that you had forgotten or never felt before.

Summon up the experience, the person, the smells, images, words, the fullness of what you touched, and as you do so continue breathing in the present moment. Notice if you start to tense up with angst or frustration or sadness. If you do, pause there, breathe, and soften. Take it slow, obeying and respecting the wisdom of your body. Relax your brow and your body, asking: What can be softer? Let emotions move, softening around them as much as you can, intending that they move through you as offerings of gratitude to life for bringing you the gift of majesty.

When you are ready, gently open your eyes and return to your physical body. Bring to mind this gift for a moment. Moving through deep intimacy with another, and even losing that intimacy, will fuel your passion and bring your life into alignment with what's most precious to you. By absorbing in this ritual way, you are reaching back and bringing the experience current, pulling whatever imagination and passion was bound up in the past into your present moment and the path ahead.

Offer It Up Ritual

Create a temporary altar or space of beauty somewhere outside your home—a place where you can feel a power greater than yourself. This could be a circle of stones and shells at the beach or by a river or a gathering of pine cones and flowers on a wooden stump in the forest or even an urban place. Bring together objects that you can endow with the positive aspects of the love you shared as in specific experiences or qualities of the person or the relationship: this flower is for the deep intimacy; this curve of a shell is the feeling of home we shared, etc.

Make it beautiful, and when it is all assembled, take a moment to speak or pray in gratitude for the gifts of the relationship that were and always will be within you and that are returning to the flow of life through you.

As you prepare to leave the altar behind and go on your way, know that you are trusting powers greater than you to hold the experiences represented in this sacred space. Releasing this way goes beyond simply trying to let go. After all, your soul will resist letting go of something that was sacred to you. But by offering it up to a greater, wiser power than your own—the forest, the ocean, or the divine presence that holds all of our lives in its hand—you allow your subconscious to release more fully.

Burying or Burning Ritual

The end of a relationship is a kind of death. Whatever dreams, possibilities, fantasies, potential love, hopes for children with that person—all these have died with the end of the relationship. You must acknowledge and grieve these things so that they can be truly at rest and you can be at peace. Create a ritual to honor and mourn the relationship.

First, bring together objects that symbolize the experience. Handle the objects with care, honoring them as you would anything beloved. You may want to add flowers, herbs, or incense to your collection. Choose whether you will bury or burn them, keeping in mind safety and ecological considerations, of course. Neither of these is in the spirit of destroying or cutting away. Burying is an act of putting to rest what is no longer living, of offering it to the care of the earth and the renewing power of growth. Burning is an act of transformation, allowing it to be converted fully into light and warmth again, returned to something more essential and less bound by form.

SEVEN

Reclaiming Your Sacred Needs

The word *sacred* has its origins in the Old French word *sacrer,* meaning to anoint or dedicate, and the older Latin word *sacrare,* meaning to consecrate or set apart. To hold something sacred, therefore, is to honor it, to recognize it as special, or to lift it up to the light. For millennia, the gifts of the feminine were hidden away in the shadows—mistaken, misunderstood, and misjudged. In the last few decades, however, many women and men have been rediscovering these gifts and stories and restoring the sacred Her to an honored place in their homes and hearts.

Despite this exciting sense of movement toward a deeper understanding of the feminine, we still live in a culture that is mostly frenetic and male driven and prioritizes mind over body and emotion. Within this landscape, many of our needs, and our deep feminine sensibility, hide in plain sight—quite literally invisible to the mainstream culture. Because of this, many of us go through life and relationships feeling conflicted at best and crazy at worst, simply because we have needs that emerge from the female body, psyche, and soul. In bringing these unique needs out from the shadow and into the light, we can anoint, honor, and cherish them, and when we honor our needs and the sacred feminine that embodies them, we honor ourselves. We make ourselves sacred.

This tension between our feminine essence and the culture at large makes it extremely common for us to pathologize our own needs—to think something is wrong with us. When a need arises within—such as one for greater honesty, connection, slowing down and nourishing our souls, or securing emotional safety—we have a tendency to doubt or invalidate it. If we do have the courage to express our need, we are likely to get a response that makes us feel wrong for having it. For example, we might be told we're being "codependent" or too needy, that we're too emotional, that we're high-maintenance or unreasonable. In all of those labels, the simplicity of what we want gets lost. In my view, this problem is rooted in a culture that doesn't understand the true value of feminine power. We've been conditioned to downplay our most basic needs. This leads to the direct result that we often stay too long in relationships that hurt us or don't fulfill us.

Imagine a world where it would be commonplace to see embodied examples of deep connection, a sense of the sacred, and honored sexuality. How revolutionary would that be? Instead, we see relationship models that prioritize excessive independence, or normalize hypersexuality, or idealize power and control. We just don't get to see the daily authentic connection that keeps love alive. Chances are you've walked away from at least one past relationship thinking your needs won't ever be met, and perhaps you've even been made to feel that these basic needs are unreasonable and unrealistic.

In this chapter we are going to cover what I refer to as *sacred needs*. To begin to explain this idea, let's contrast sacred needs with what you might call your personality needs. For instance, on the level of personality, you might feel that you need someone who is extroverted (or introverted), who likes the same things you like, who abstains from substances (or doesn't), who is tall, has a stable job, is a particular age, lives near you, doesn't (or does) have children, etc. Many "needs" at this level are just ideas of what you think might be right for you, and life often brings us opportunities to see beyond them. We might call these needs, but it's more accurate to describe them as preferences or desires.

Sacred needs, on the other hand, are those things that bring you true fulfillment in your relationships and sustain you in your personal power. Sacred needs are absolutely necessary for an authentically empowered and balanced relationship. Knowing what your sacred needs are, as well as knowing how to express and articulate them, is a crucial feminine art that will bring harmony to your inner world. In this way, your sacred needs are a gift you bring to your relationship, not a demanding strain you put on your relationship.

The Five Universal Needs

While you will have an evolving list of your sacred needs, I would like to share with you what I consider to be the five feminine universal sacred needs:

1. To be seen

2. To be met

3. To trust/to be held

4. To be protected

5. To be cherished

As we look together at these sacred needs, you may find that others become clear within you. If so, hold the revelation of these needs as a sacred gift and give them space in your world. Your deep needs are not wrong, or needy, or weird, or too much. They are a part of what makes you who you are and should be honored as such.

The sacred need *to be seen* means being perceived all the way down to your essential nature. When someone sees you in this way, we could say that they bring your soul to the surface. Your intimate partner is one of the closest people to you, and your deep connection can only occur if you feel like you are being seen by him or her. You may have already experienced what it feels like not to be seen, if in your past loverships there was a veil or image you hid behind or a projection on the part of your partner where they saw what they wanted to see instead of who you really were. When you recognize this sacred need and its importance for deep connection, you will naturally only allow in those people who really see you.

The sacred need *to be met* is more than just a physical interaction; it describes a real encounter of the heart and mind on an energetic level. For this reason, it's not always easy to describe this need. Certainly it includes a partner who is willing to listen to you and try to understand how you feel about things, but it is even more than that. When someone meets you fully and receives your energy, you open like a rose, and you lift your being up to send and receive more of that precious energy. I hear a lot of women talk about "not feeling heard, understood, or met," and what they are really missing is a sacred meeting that occurs on a soul level. It can take time for someone to meet you at this level, but if that depth is not reached and you stay on the surface, there will always be a longing in the most essential part of you.

The sacred need *to trust* (or the need to be held) is necessary in part so that you can surrender. Surrendering physically, sexually, and emotionally requires a trustworthy person holding the energetic space for you to step into, and you need to know that you will be cared for rather than hurt. The feminine being desires the ecstasy of surrender, but in her deepest wisdom she will not fully surrender unless there is someone trustworthy to receive her. Without that trust, you will feel isolated, insecure, and unsafe.

There are places the feminine soul can only touch through surrender. Your need to trust, and to be energetically held, is nonnegotiable.

Related to the need to trust is a sacred need *to be protected*. You need to know that your partner has your back in ways that might be physical, mental, emotional, or even spiritual. Remember, while we all have our personal power, there are also times in which we are vulnerable. That's why I describe the divine essence of woman as a unique combination of power and vulnerability. Power tempered by vulnerability has a necessary integrity and humility. The need to be protected is not a sign of weakness, as there will also be times when you need to protect and have the back of your partner. Vulnerabilities are a part of authentic power, they reflect the true nature of our existence. Finding a partner who protects your vulnerabilities is an absolute need for the relationship to grow.

A final sacred need is *to be cherished*. While this is similar to what some may call appreciation, cherishing goes even deeper. Being cherished brings your deep feminine essence to the surface. The opposite of cherish in this context is neglect, and so many of us know how that feels. In my experience, being cherished goes beyond simply feeling good. It is how the heart and soul of the partnership thrive; it is love made manifest.

Needs Can Seem Weird

These are the core sacred needs, and you may have more. You can recognize sacred needs because they won't go away and they touch a deep longing in you, one that may even seem irrational. Remember, sacred needs are not about what you like or don't like, what's acceptable in society, or what you should or shouldn't be "satisfied" with. Rather, sacred needs are the rich soil in which love deepens, grows, and opens.

There's an old story about a rock band on tour. Their contract included wildly excessive demands for the venues they were to play in, one of which was that a bowl of only green M&Ms must be in their dressing room. After many years of keeping quiet as they were ridiculed for this diva behavior, the band finally came clean with the reason for this request. Because of the weight of the equipment for their performance setup, there was a real danger at many venues that the stage could collapse, putting staff and audiences in mortal danger. All of the technical specifications were detailed in their contract, but the band's managers knew that venues don't always read the fine print. So, if they walked in and the green

M&Ms were not there, it was a good sign that the contracts had not been read and it would not be safe to perform. Safety, in this case, was the deep need—and the "weird" demand for green M&Ms was totally valid and not outrageous in the least.

Claiming and honoring your sacred needs are the way to find your path forward into current or future intimacies that actually nourish you, that meet or exceed your imaginings, that don't abandon, betray, or neglect your feminine essence. Clearing ex-lovers not only frees you from the past; it opens the door to what will be.

As an example, as I was recovering from an important relationship, I realized that one of my sacred needs was to feel contained. In order for me to fully surrender to love, to open completely, and to know the fullness of my own pleasure, I needed containment. I needed to feel closely held in a closed circle with my partner. In order to share myself and my sexuality with self-respect and the level of surrender that I desire, I need a high level of sexual fidelity and focus. I understand now that what makes me feel seen, met, cherished, and safe enough to be vulnerable is to feel very closely held. Not trapped, but held. My need for a very committed, very sexually faithful and exclusive relationship is not based on jealousy, insecurity, or an idea about what I think is best. It is a sacred need and one that must be met in order for me to flower. I discovered this through hardship, but I was then able to bring it to my current relationship and have it met, honored, and cherished as a part of me. It has opened the door to a kind of sweet, passionate, and secure intimacy I have never known before and that I had been hopeless about ever experiencing.

What's more, over time I have realized that the sacred need of containment that I discovered through the hardship of my relationship carries over into the rest of my life. In general, I flourish when I feel contained. I am stronger when I keep my energy close to myself. I am more functional if I keep my focus close on projects, one at a time. The practices that nourish me the most are those that seal up my energy field. Not all of us are this way. Some will flourish with greater space, a lot of stimulation, or an expansive horizon. I do find, however, that the sacred needs you have in sexual intimacy lie at the core essence of your true nature. Sexual intimacy touches the heart of things, and it is there that you can discover secrets that will help you thrive in all aspects of your life.

Sacred Womanhood

If you have been in a relationship in which sacred needs were not met, you most likely experienced confusion when trying to relate emotionally to your partner. You might have felt an acute sense of shallowness or like something was missing. On the other hand, if you found the meeting of sacred needs with someone and started to open and blossom, but then lost the intimacy, you may have found yourself exposed and feeling more vulnerable than ever.

As you move forward, remember that even if you still feel very enmeshed with a former partner, you need nothing from your relationship of the past. You are not crazy, broken, needy, or overwhelming. You're just a woman, and inside of you are sacred needs that point the way toward harmony, reciprocity, and a blending of sexuality, emotion, heart, and soul that is one of the greatest expressions of human relationship.

When you consciously make sacred needs an honored part of your experience as a woman, rather than an aspect of yourself to fear or avoid, they will bring you into the fullness of what you were created to be. The fulfillment of longing is contained within longing itself. You must allow yourself to long for what you truly love, so that your longing can bring you what you have always desired.

Your Nonnegotiables

Once you are in touch with your sacred needs, you will have the self-knowledge to establish your non-negotiables.

Nonnegotiables are the things you are not willing to compromise. When you are clear with yourself about what these are for you, they become the bedrock of your power to discern and to make good choices for yourself. For many of us, it's only after we experience the pain of compromising our non-negotiables that they become clear to us. The highest cost we ever pay is that of betraying ourselves, and in my experience once this happens you truly know what is fundamentally sacred to you. In other words, even self-betrayal becomes a chance for you to be a trustworthy guardian of your values.

In my case, it wasn't until the end of my seven-year relationship that I understood one of my most fundamental nonnegotiables: I simply didn't want to be in a sexual relationship with someone who couldn't hold my version of sexual fidelity with me. Until that point, I had tried everything—processing my insecurities, attempting to be more "sex positive," going to couples therapy and personal therapy, and practicing ritual. I tried on disempowering perceptions of myself, thinking that perhaps I was a prude, or broken, or madly insecure, or that I simply just wasn't woman enough. I did everything I could to make it about me, internalize it, and try to change, to become something "better." No matter what I did or tried, nothing worked.

Exhausted with this self-abuse masquerading as self-improvement, I finally stopped. I returned to where I started. I needed a partner who could hold my version of sexual fidelity with me. I deserved to feel good, be nourished, and come alive. It wasn't because I was broken or insecure or a prude; it was because I valued honor and fidelity, and nothing I did could make the relationship into something it wasn't.

The cost of learning this was high, but the power I received from this wisdom was even higher. I came out of that relationship literally unable to violate what was sacred to me. It took seven years, but I had finally exhausted all of my secret, unconscious reasons for betraying my own values—and I was left with the simple reality of my nonnegotiable values that I cannot compromise or amend without violating my deepest nature.

Now I understand it: I require complete and passionate sexual fidelity from my chosen intimate partner. It's plain and simple, nonnegotiable. It's not an option, and anything other than that will cost more than it gives. I know that from experience now, and nothing can make me doubt myself or my values. When you know your nonnegotiables *and you cease questioning them and doubting yourself*, you become a formidable ally to your soul and a much better partner, because you are clear on what is best for you.

Action Steps

Let's identify your sacred needs and nonnegotiables with the journal prompts and exercises below.

Exploring Your Sacred Needs

In your journal, I invite you to respond to this prompt:

What I need to fully open into love is . . .

Try not to edit your responses based on what you've known in past relationships or what you think is possible for you now or in the future. Really dive into picturing the most idyllic, whole, full expression of love in the universe. Don't hold back. Your needs might be similar to one of the universal sacred needs.

You will know when you've identified a sacred need because it will bring your soul to the surface. It will guide you to create intimacies that are passionate but safe, secure and honoring, but exciting and alive. Your knowledge and intimacy with your sacred needs are the greatest gift you can bring to future relationships and the greatest guarantee you can have of avoiding relationships that will never meet your needs. Remember that need, sacred need in particular, has its own fulfillment hidden inside of it. Bringing your sacred needs to life will bring your desires for a healthy sexual relationship to fruition.

Determining Your Nonnegotiables

Next, I invite you to do some writing that will uncover your nonnegotiables. Start with the following prompts, and feel free to keep going in whatever direction they take you. Challenge yourself to get down to the core values.

- ♥ What has been your biggest issue in your past relationships? What comes up for you again and again?

- ♥ What do you know now that you could never have known with such confidence

before you went through the difficulties
of your past relationship?

♥ Now and in the future what do you
require, not desire?

The answers to these questions will be specific
to you, forged by your own past suffering. These
answers, the nonnegotiable values of your deepest
nature, form the sword in the hand of your guardianship. Nothing and no one can get close to you
without passing the test of your uncompromising
self-respect. You can stand tall and strong behind
what is nonnegotiable for you and allow relationships to either rise to the occasion or fall away.

EIGHT

Creating Boundaries for Future Loverships

I once had a misunderstanding with a dear friend about boundaries. We had been spending time together, shopping for lovely things, and having a blast. The next day, she had a regret hangover about one of her purchases, and she was pretty sure it was my fault. She had confided in me about her chronic over-spending and her never-ending debt. I should have known that she really didn't want to spend money, she argued, and I should have been a better friend. I gently reminded her how much fun we have together no matter what we're doing and affirmed that she's in charge of her own decisions. Of course, the one who failed to uphold her boundaries was herself, not me, but it felt easier in the moment to put the responsibility anywhere but on her own shoulders. "I'm just so frustrated about the way I keep spending more than I have, no matter how much I try to stop," she complained, as she sobered up and took responsibility for her own actions. I'm happy to say we quickly worked it out, but it was a simple example of how easy it can be to violate our own boundaries and then immediately direct the blame elsewhere.

We hear a lot of talk about boundaries in the context of relationships these days, which in my view can make boundaries seem more complicated than they are. They are often invoked as a cover for selfish or exclusive behavior (just as false "self-love" can be an excuse for plain old narcissism). While articulating and maintaining strong boundaries can take work, the core is simple: boundaries are just what's okay and what's not okay. Many people think of boundaries as walls, which creates resistance to making and keeping them. Who wants to block themselves off from the people and things they love or imprison their energy in a fortress?

I prefer to think of boundaries as a home rather than a wall—one that has windows, doors, and bright, sunny patios. I can open the doors and shut them as

I wish, and it's quite obvious to friends and strangers alike that it's not okay to come in through the window or bust through a wall with a sledgehammer. Without boundaries, I am in a sense homeless. My space is not my own, and it takes most of my physical and mental energy just to stay safe, warm, and fed. Surviving is so chaotic and taxing that I cannot do anything else. See the difference?

When you've built a home with someone else physically, mentally, emotionally, and energetically, the ending of that relationship can feel like a tornado has blown through. Only when you have restored appropriate and healthy boundaries can you break the grip of the relationship. You must reorient yourself to what it is to be singular, no longer unified with another. For many of us there is a mixture of grief and relief in this process. It's sad to let go of what was loved, but in many cases it's also a relief to finally be free of dynamics that were draining, unfulfilling, or hopeless.

If you've been feeling caught in unresolved feelings and thought patterns about a past relationship, restoring boundaries is a crucial step in recovery. The way to do this is to maintain your focus on foundational personal power, rather than the story that continues to replay in your mind. To be clear, reestablishing boundaries is not about things such as who gets what when, whose money is whose, who gets the kids when, and all the other external practicalities that must be sorted out. These details are obviously important, but they are a *reflection* of fundamentally healthy boundaries within you. The truth is that until you create good boundaries on the inside, external boundaries will only keep up the illusion that healthy agreements are in place, while in reality you are actually still as entangled and enmeshed as you ever were.

It seems simple, and so obvious, that we need to bring our energy back inside us and create a healthy boundary for our own well-being. Of course simple is not always easy—if it were, you and I and so many of us would be free of ongoing confusion and bouts of anger, bitterness, and other unresolved feelings that come up again and again. Often we find our minds preoccupied with our former partners and the new life they may be living, and on an emotional and energetic level we experience an unending heart-break about the past.

Healthy boundaries are not something you decide to have simply because it's a good idea; they are necessary to protect the personal power you are reclaiming and key to maintaining your sexual sovereignty going forward.

Like your home, boundaries are a living presence and protection around you that you must tend and keep sound. True boundaries that move according to deep feminine essence will bring you back to life. Contrary to some popular ideas about boundaries, they do not separate you from life or make you rigid, narcissistic, bitter, or any other negative quality. True boundaries actually make you *more* connected to life and others. The difference is you are conscious about what parts of yourself you share, with whom, and on what terms.

There are three things to consider when setting boundaries in your life that feel good to you, that bring you back to life, that free you from constant conflict with the past (or present), and that you can maintain regardless of the attitudes or behavior of others.

Boundaries focus on keeping you in rather than keeping others out. If there were one revolutionary statement about boundaries that I could plaster everywhere, it would be this. It is based on a core principle of deep feminine sovereignty, which is that the safest place you can be is full of your essence, intimate with your truth, and honestly listening to your true sacred needs. The only way to cultivate this level of self-knowing and empowerment is to stay close to yourself, to focus on nurturing your power, and to keep your energy for you, first and foremost.

When you shift to holding boundaries as a way to keep you in rather than to keep others out, you turn the whole conversation on its head, in the best way. First of all, you shift your focus to the place you are going to actually have the most influence—in some ways the only place you have any influence—yourself. You can't control anyone else; you already know you can't change what you've experienced with past lovers and of course you can't demand that life provide you with someone who fits every one of your desires. But you *can* choose again and again to know yourself more deeply, to cultivate your energy and power, and to learn your inner terrain so that you can make choices that really serve you.

Healthy boundaries are semipermeable. This means that you welcome what you know to be good for you, while keeping out that which does not serve you. Just like the doors in your house, you get to choose when to open, at what time, in what mood, and to whom. As you process your past relationships and reclaim your power, you will have taken stock of what's important to you and what you really want. As you start to trust your intuition, the process of letting in what's good for you begins to occur naturally. When you sense an offering that comes from the right intention and energy, you welcome it. When you feel that what is being offered isn't genuine, or is manipulative, or comes with "strings attached," the doors of your energy slam shut and keep it out. In this way, the only people who will be able to stay in your life and form a deep intimate bond with you are the ones who can pass through this semipermeable membrane.

Finally, *boundaries are alive.* Healthy boundaries are not rigid or conceptual; they aren't what you will always do or never do or what you have locked onto as the "best way." In fact, the saying "never say never" points to the fact that a harsh boundary is more likely to be breached than a flexible one. You are a living creature who is always changing, and you get to make boundaries that are living and responsive as well. As you create boundaries and agreements that support your well-being and your growth away from the dysfunctional dynamics of past relationships, remember that flexible boundaries can adapt to circumstance and therefore maintain themselves. Of course you will maintain the nonnegotiables you articulated in the last chapter, but the realms of sexuality, passion, the heart, and the soul are fluid, alive, and wild, and for this reason your boundaries may adjust, grow, and change depending on the situation.

As you nurture yourself and your energy, you will find that the boundaries you create have an intelligence of their own. In this way we could say that your boundaries are *principled*, but not fixed. From a place of principles, you can respond in the moment to the details of each unique situation, based on what you're actually feeling and the energy of the moment, rather than getting into an exhausting mental defense of a conceptual boundary. Life will present you with new and interesting situations and people, and if you hold tight to your ideas about what *should* be happening or how things *should* be, you cut off your ability to learn and grow, not to mention your intuitive wisdom about what to do with what *is* happening.

In this way, boundaries help you trust yourself more. It's exhausting to defend a fortress of rigid boundaries around yourself that say, "This person must do this, or say this, or agree with me on this, or fit a certain preconceived idea I have to be in my life." Healthy boundaries are alive and intelligent and can respond to new circumstances in whatever way will best serve your well-being. None of us has all the answers about life, and this is especially true in the area of intimate relationships, so by having principled boundaries rather than rigid ones, we can allow them to grow and change in ways that serve our evolving well-being.

You have probably built most of your rigid opinions or perceptions about what is right or wrong as a result of pain and loss. It's time to soften those and lay them to rest. Like all the other residual impacts of former lovers, they don't benefit your present existence. Don't worry—you are not letting go of your knowledge of what's okay and what's not okay. You simply get to define your new intimacies not as a reaction to past negative experiences, but by opening to boundaries that keep your spine strong and your heart soft.

Creating Positive Boundaries

Your boundaries are positive, not negative, and for this reason your focus should be on what you want instead of what you don't want. That brings your emphasis to the positive and keeps you open to change, learning, and, most importantly, freedom from the past.

As a way to bring these ideas together, I'd like to share the story of one of my clients and her journey to creating boundaries that were focused on nurturing her own inner power, allowing in what was good for her, and opening to evolution and change according to the wisdom of life. I began working with her about six months after she ended a three-year relationship, one in which she experienced a fair amount of neglect. I could tell that this past lover still had his grip on her, as the boundaries she was creating in the present were mostly reactions against this relationship.

For instance, one of the first things she explained was that she would not engage sexually with another man until he came to her fully ready for a long-term relationship. This was a new boundary for her, and it was in reaction to the way she had started her previous relationship. In addition, she had very clear ideas about how this new boundary would manifest and the type of man she would look for as a result. He would know that he wanted a long-term relationship, and he would express that to her in words and deeds. In addition, because she felt that part of the problem with her past lover was that he was "younger and unsettled," she only wanted an older man, one who was financially secure. As you can see, she had very strong expectations in place, and she felt like the new boundaries that she had set were absolutely in her best interest.

The first problem with this plan was that after a few months of only dating men who fit these criteria, she was not experiencing a spark or true connection with anyone. As time went on, she became frustrated at not being able to express her sexuality. In short, she had created rigid boundaries and very clear opinions about what would be best for her, but it was backfiring. She felt trapped, unsatisfied, and because her boundaries were in reaction to her past lover, she was still effectively bound to him. As we worked together and she looked more deeply, she saw that her new boundaries didn't originate from her own centered, wise discernment. Of course she never wanted to experience that level of neglect again, and for good reason she felt very protective of herself—but her boundaries, though well-meaning, were ultimately arising from her distrust of herself. As you can see by now, these boundaries were based on outside rules that kept others out, rather than inside principles that kept her energy intact.

After we talked and got clearer about where her boundaries were actually coming from, she was able to pull out of the reactive cycle to her former lover, return to her center, and establish a true sense of self-authority. She restored trust in herself and realized that she had learned what she needed to from that relationship. She would never allow neglect like that again. She could allow herself the freedom to experience what life would bring, whether or not it fit her narrow concepts of what "safe" and "cherished" should look like.

She shed her rigid external boundaries and entered a chapter of life that was incredibly rich. She went on dates with a variety of men, some of them many years younger than she was. She began a phase of exploration that not only broke the spell of her previous relationship, but also taught her how deeply she could trust her own intuition to know and express, "Yes, this is for me," or "No, thank you."

My client's boundaries shifted from rigid reactions based on a past experience to a source of living discernment that allowed her to embrace life, trust herself, and have a variety of new adventures. She learned to allow her "yes" and her "no" to arise in the moment, and it wasn't long before her feminine essence began to thrive. She realized that she didn't need to exhaust herself by trying to control every man who came near her. Instead, by feeling free and alive again, her own wisdom inside could grow, flower, and lead her in moments of decision that would keep her safe and cherished always.

One thing I hope you can glean from this example is that it is essential, especially in intimate relationships, for outward rules to flow from inward principles. Having rigid boundaries for their own sake leads you to either shut down to new experience or to break your boundaries and then feel bad about yourself. Semipermeable boundaries allow you to honor your core values while remaining open to creative, spontaneous possibilities in the future.

When it comes to relationships, don't sell yourself short by attempting black-and-white rules only. It's okay for there to be nuance. That doesn't in any way mean that you have to allow in what hurts or confuses you, but by being focused on the positive, open to learning something new, and committed to nurturing your own energy and deep feminine essence, you will naturally keep out what is toxic.

Renewing Trust in Yourself and Others

Without boundaries, we cannot fully trust. As we have discussed, a big reason past relationships linger with us is that we experienced a break in trust. Our past lover's breach of trust often gets much of the attention in our mind, but we also need to contend with the boundaries we break with ourselves and the resulting loss of trust. Depending on the circumstances by which the relationship ends, we may lose faith in our ability to see what's actually going on, to make good choices, or we may beat ourselves up for being in a relationship with this person in the first place. Remember, it's a warrior's journey to surrender into trust and to develop relationships of trust. It requires bravery, persistence, and the ability to get up time and time again in the face of apparent defeat. And it absolutely requires your trust in your own sword—your discernment—and your own capacity for total restoration, regardless of wounds received.

Until you focus on harvesting the wisdom from past loverships, lack of trust and faith in yourself can turn into a subtly jaded state of being. It is the process of accumulating self-knowledge through apparent relationship failures that will shift your experience of yourself from powerless to powerful. Because sexual intimacy touches some of the most vulnerable terrain inside us, loss of confidence in ourselves can spill over into other areas and can affect our trust in life and trust in other people generally.

There are many ways you can and will address the rebuilding of trust in your life, from therapy to friendships, art and self-expression, and new and healthier intimacies. In addition to all of these, as you endeavor to reckon with ways that your innate trust in life has been impacted by a past relationship, I invite you to approach the restoration of trust as one more layer of initiation.

Much like the fabled loss of innocence, the loss of trust can feel irreversible. In a way, it is. You can no longer rest in the naive assumption that honesty is a given or that integrity will be upheld by people close to you, or that if you do your best, love will triumph over all. In order to initiate fully through the loss of trust, you must go on a journey, from naivety into suffering, loss of self, and finally the wisdom only gained through experience.

Strong and balanced boundaries release your need to control others—which never ultimately works, at least not for very long. The irony is that the best way to influence the health of a relationship with another is to take care of yourself, honoring your wisdom and self-knowing. Rather than trying to control another, when you reclaim your power and maintain your sexual sovereignty, you magnetize what you really want and allow intimacies to deepen rather than collapse and wither away. The relative ease and natural grace of releasing control in order to have a healthy influence for the good depend directly on creating personal boundaries that are living and responsive, protective without being aggressive.

When you honor your own needs, you will find that other people in your life will instinctively do the same. Over time, you will shift from relationships based on negotiation—where defensiveness and resentment are the norm—to relationships grounded in reciprocity, in which you can be forthright about needs and wants in a natural back-and-forth that feeds both partners.

Action Steps

The following ritual brings the intellectual understanding you have gained of healthy boundaries into your body through a deep visualization practice.

Creating Your Vessel

Return to the place you have created where you feel calm and will be undisturbed for at least twenty to thirty minutes. Take a few minutes to simply breathe, sending relaxing energy into any parts of your body that feel tense or tight.

Once you are settled in, imagine a vessel surrounding you. This might take any form—a beautiful golden bowl, a flowering plant, or even a floating bubble of air and light. Feel your body inside this vessel, supported and contained. Let this image delight you and take its own shape. Notice what colors or shapes your vessel takes in your awareness.

As you connect deeper, feel how your body interacts with this vessel. Does it warm your skin? Bear all of your weight with softness, or firm support? Is it cool to the touch, like the stones in an ancient temple? Let your body take on these feeling as you set your imagination free.

Next, envision a few ways that your vessel is semipermeable. It might be a magical shape-shifter, a cloud that parts for the sun and closes again, the loving arms of a goddess. Your vessel is fluid, and even as it adapts to your body and your needs, it always holds you and protects you.

Within this vessel, envision how your energy, your vitality, your personal power, and your sexual sovereignty all converge as the nectar within you. Again, go as far as you can into feeling this in your body. Is there a sweetness to this nectar? A temperature? A color? As you create the vessel that will always hold you, remember that the sacred function of boundaries is to protect what is most treasured and essential.

Envision your vessel as the protector and guardian of not only your energetic nectar, but also your attention and your time. It protects you against depletions of energy, and from putting your attention on things that do not serve you. Inside this vessel you nourish your own energy and you do not look to anyone else to fill you up. Feel the sensations of fullness and what it is to be truly present and anchored in your own energy. For anyone who would attempt to violate or challenge your boundaries, the strength and protection of your vessel will easily turn them away.

Lastly, envision being joined in this sacred space by your current or future partner, with whom you will cultivate relationships of reciprocity and mutual respect. You might even be able to envision their vessel—totally different from yours and yet complementary, holding and protecting their strength and energy, while remaining open to you. In this dance of give-and-take, boundaries are a natural living part of the way both of you protect the relationship, rather than guard yourselves against each other.

Stay in this place as long as you like. Feel the energy. When you are ready, gently open your eyes and return to your physical body.

Return here anytime you feel depleted or like your energy is flowing away from you.

NINE

Establishing Your Sexual Sovereignty

Long before it was shamed by culture and religious misunderstanding, female sexuality was revered. But long-standing cultural misperceptions persist, so female sexuality today is feared, controlled, and marginalized. As a result, you may encounter fear of your sexuality, or you may have internalized shame about your feminine power. This is normal, but misguided. Fully embodied female sexual potency is *not* an inappropriately seductive, hypersexualized, or manipulative force. Such expressions of "sexuality" are really just symptoms of misplaced power that leave negative energy in their place.

What I've seen in myself—and in almost every single woman I've had the privilege of working with—is that we rarely, if ever, have gone into a relationship with a true sense of sexual sovereignty. As such, there's no chance we could have truly navigated the power and vulnerabilities of sexual intimacy. This is not surprising when you consider the culture we grew up in, which doesn't honor, or even understand, the true nature of female sexuality. In fact, I would go as far as to say that it has been hijacked and misrepresented in most cases, and at the very least it has been invalidated. Even in those rare instances where a female was raised with a strong sense of self-authority and honor about her sexuality, she too has likely had difficulty claiming her sexual sovereignty in a relationship.

This makes sense, since every sexually intimate relationship is different and you will react differently to each one. Sexual relationships themselves are sometimes the only place to understand certain hidden vulnerabilities that motivate you: the places where you give yourself away, the places where you long to be met but simultaneously fear the surrender that such a meeting would require.

In order to fully clear past lovers, it is essential that you realize your sexual fire is your own. When you come to know your deep feminine essence in your body, not just your mind, you'll come to sexual intimacies with far greater discernment, greater capacity for pleasure, and a real chance at nourishing a sexual relationship that brings good into your world.

In past relationships, you may have shaped your sexual needs and desires to the limitations of your partner. That may have even worked, at least in the short run, but as you know by now, this type of behavior almost never leaves you filled up for very long. When you establish your sexual sovereignty, you are able to shape your future relationships to *your* needs and desires and form a clear picture of what is and is not good for you.

When you start to experience the fullness of your sexual energy, make decisions with that in mind, and cultivate that energy on an ongoing basis, you'll put an end to any previous tendencies you may have had to settle in unfulfilling sexual relationships just for the sake of being in one or to tolerate dysfunction just for the sake of keeping one going. Once you reclaim your sexual sovereignty, your sense of your power as a woman will be far more fulfilling and delicious.

Remember as you explore this that there is no right or wrong way to be sexual; there is only your way. Stay connected with yourself and with the true intimacy that lives in you. Furthermore, this exploration is never done. As your sexuality evolves, so will your authentic connection with your sovereignty.

While the clearing and reclaiming work you have done has placed you firmly on the path of reclaiming your personal power and establishing your sexual sovereignty, it's time to go even deeper and examine three practices that will help you fully step into your own:

1. Recovering your sexual energy

2. Developing your discernment

3. Cultivating your sexual nature

Recovering Your Sexual Energy

The place to begin is with recovering the fullness of your sexual energy. This isn't just about your sex drive—it's much bigger than that. Let's start by dismissing the commonly held idea that sexuality is just in the bedroom or even explicitly sexual. Female sexuality is actually a creative force that moves along a continuum throughout many aspects of your life. Yes, it's what fuels your passion for lovemaking—but it also fuels the creativity that helps you do and build so many other things, such as raise your children, launch a business, make art, or be of service to others. When your sexual energy is drained, all of these things become more difficult and wearing. Sexual energy in this sense can also be described as a feeling of aliveness, fullness, or inspiration.

In my view, one of the greatest disservices done to female sexuality has been the trapping of this massive creative force into a strictly sexual box. Not only does female sexuality span a continuum of expression; it is also deeply influenced by many things that aren't explicitly sexual. You have undoubtedly experienced this already, as everything from being upset with your partner to dealing with normal life stress situations to an imbalance in your eating and sleeping patterns can have a direct impact on libido.

Think for a moment about your own life. If you expand your definition of sexual energy to include all the creative things you do, what would be included? You may find a new list of things that actually turn you on (or off). For instance, being creative in some fashion—playing music, sculpting, cooking, dancing, practicing deep meditation, or giving yourself intense self-care—can ignite your sexual energy. Anything that opens you, that fills your cup and feels good for your body, counts here. Looking at art, baths, walks, dates with friends, spiritual practices, massages, and naps are just a few examples. The things you do to nurture and create connection all tap into the innate power of female sexuality. It's not always about *doing* something, either. Often what depletes your sexual energy is stress, and you can usually reduce stress by doing less.

Developing Discernment

The next step to establishing your sexual sovereignty is discernment. Think about it this way: the moment you are attracted to someone sexually, there are emotional, biochemical, and spiritual processes that engage to create bonding. Discernment is about knowing whether or not that bonding is best for you, with this person, in this way, and at this time. The capacity to wisely discern whom to share your sexuality with and in what ways is a necessary skill to develop so that you don't find yourself rushing in too fast or participating in things you aren't comfortable with, diminishing your personal power in the process.

Discernment is simple in concept, but it takes time to develop. In the most basic sense, discernment is the answer to the simple question: Is this for me or not for me? It's hard because healthy discernment is often compromised by the tendency many of us have to prioritize our partner's needs over our own, as well as to judge ourselves and those around us. If you do this regularly, you may even lose touch with what you really want. The good news is that discernment lives in the body and speaks in very specific ways—so if you learn to listen, your body will send you signals in the form of feelings or intuitive nudges that will tell you if something is meant for you or not.

To see this type of discernment in action, let's look to some of the experiences in your past, this time with the benefit of hindsight. Did your body send you warning signs when you became involved in things that were not quite right for you? Did your stomach tense or turn? Did you get anxious in the moment? Did your heart clench? After the experience passed, did you have trouble sleeping or have disturbing dreams? Now that you can see more clearly what dynamics were happening and how things ultimately played out, you can review these internal signals and be on the lookout for them the next time they arise. Your signals will answer the question: Is this for me or not for me?

To be clear, discernment isn't just something you pull out when it's time to decide if you should sleep with someone or not. Discernment functions broadly as a form of self-advocacy, self-care, and guardianship of your energy that you want to bring to every aspect of your life, but especially your intimate relationships. Harvest your past intimacies for your own signals of discernment, keep them close to you always, and listen to them with respect. They are your closest lifelong allies.

Cultivating Your Sexual Nature

The final step is cultivation. Once you have connected with your sexual energy, the force that keeps you vibrant and magnetic, attractive, and open to life, you can't take it for granted. Your sexuality is a living thing, and she needs to be cultivated. Think of her as a flower that grows and opens in you. What in your life nourishes this energy? What brings you simple pleasure, relaxes you, draws heat and aliveness into your body, makes you smile, or comforts you? These things will be different for each of us. You *must* find these special things and do them regularly.

Most women neglect cultivating their sexual energy due to a combination of social pressures, life circumstances, or the habit of putting their partner's needs ahead of their own. Some women I know have even slipped into relationships that didn't serve their highest good simply because these relationships activated the sexual energy inside them that had been starving for expression and nurturance. This is also why a past sexual relationship that *was* fulfilling and positive in this area alone can continue to pull on you into the present. You can cultivate what you liked about a past relationship in your current or future partnership, too. Follow your pleasure. Nurture your body. Feed your soul. Keep it simple.

Action Steps
Growing Your Garden

There are many ways to enrich your sexual sovereignty beyond explicit sexual acts. Be creative in your thinking, and feel into the following statement on an energetic level:

What cultivates my sexual energy is . . .

What activities help you feel clear, alive, and strong? This could be a creative practice, a spiritual practice, etc. It helps to imagine your sexual current, your feminine essence, as a nectar that you hold, or even a river that runs through you. What nourishes that nectar in you? What fills the banks of your river? What do you turn to when you run dry? Write your answers in your journal.

Now turn to the inverse of this statement:

What depletes my sexual energy is . . .

Take a moment to consider all that diminishes your sexual energy. For instance, if you don't take time for self-care, you may find your sexual energy is depleted as a result. Sit with this for a few minutes and write down all the ways you can lower your sexual energy, as knowing what to avoid can be just as important as understanding what nourishes you.

With these two lists in front of you, make a plan for one thing you can do this week to cultivate your sexual energy. Also set a reminder to check in with yourself midweek to see if you've slipped into any old habits that deplete your sexual energy. How can you replace those behaviors with new habits that will nurture this side of you?

Water Bearer Practice

This next practice will help you to connect more deeply with sexual energy, discernment, and cultivation. Some of you may recognize the water bearer as the symbol for the astrological sign Aquarius, but the meaning of the water bearer is one who gives life and spiritual nourishment to the world.

To start, return to your place that is quiet, comfortable, and undisturbed, giving yourself about twenty minutes for this practice. Close your eyes, center on your breathing, and soften your body, your brow, your heart, and your belly. Imagine your sexual energy as water that flows within you, and let it show itself to you in color, shape, element, fragrance, or any other sensual ways. Does your sexual current seem bright or dim, big or small, made of flame or water, hot or cold? For this first connection, you just want to get a sense of it in its essential form.

Once you feel centered and you've deepened the breath, ask yourself the following questions of your sexual energy, one at a time:

1. Am I frozen? And if so, where?

2. Am I stagnant? And if so, where?

3. Am I leaking? And if so, where?

Allow each answer to reveal itself through your body rather than your mind. You may find that you really feel one of these more than the others, or you may find ways in which all three are present in your body. Don't beat yourself up or try to "fix" anything. Just notice, listen, watch, and be curious.

If you discovered frozen places, imagine yourself breathing warmth into them and melting the cold. If you discovered stagnancies, imagine bringing the flow of fresh water and movement to these areas. If you found places that leak, seal them up, bringing strength and containment. When you are ready, gently open your eyes and return to your physical body.

Remember, like some of the meditations and rituals from earlier in the book, this is deep energetic work, and the changes here occur beyond the level of the conscious mind. Overall, these questions give you a sense of where your sexual energy is right now and what your tendencies toward imbalance are. If you found mostly frozen places, most likely your tendency is to become cold and rigid and to shut down. If you found stagnant places, you likely tend to go dormant and become heavy and unresponsive or listless. If you found leaky places, you are probably spilling sexual energy in unconscious ways in order to be seen, to receive attention, and to feel safe.

These protective mechanisms are misguided, because when your sexual current freezes, stagnates, or leaks out of you, you actually become more vulnerable and less safe. You have fewer of your own resources available to you. Discernment and cultivation will help you to protect yourself without closing down or losing energy, so that you have full access to your power.

If you find the water bearer practice beneficial, then I suggest doing it on a regular basis, as it can help you address imbalances as they arise in your sexual energy. It is supremely empowering to learn about your sexual energy in this way, without a partner or an external circumstance to excite or disturb it. Not only will it keep recovering any losses that happened in your past relationship, but it will also bring you self-awareness that you can carry into any future relationship. Fostering sexual sovereignty will change everything in your present moment, and revolutionize the kind of sexual intimacies you'll create in the future.

Conclusion

As you may have noticed, the process of clearing past lovers has very little to do with them or what happened in the past, but is instead very much about you and what you are doing right now in the present.

When you understand a past relationship in the larger context of personal initiation, you see that it doesn't have to be an unfortunate loss or a tragic chapter in the book of your life. It becomes a necessary and honored part of your own evolution into the woman you were created to be. You can—and you will—become even more of yourself on the other side of this initiation, regardless of what impacts still linger or how hopeless it seems to have become.

As you continue to break the lingering spells of any past lovers, you will likely be surprised by both your resilience and the tenacity with which some patterns hold on. Some things won't release until their own timing is met, until you have received all that there is to receive from them.

If old dynamics creep back in or if a preoccupation with "what could have been" or how you could have done better gets loud, remember that the first thing to do is resist the urge to pathologize. There's nothing wrong, broken, or bad happening. It is natural and normal for sexual intimacies to unravel over time, for emotionally intense connections to resolve layer by layer, for the grief of losing a relationship to come in waves. So if you find yourself in looping thoughts, helpless anger, hopelessness, or preoccupation with a former lover, keep the following plan of action on hand for emergency recovery and realignment:

- *Turn* your full attention toward yourself.

- *Find* the sacred need under the surface.

- *Breathe* with it, and let it come to life in you.

- *Honor* it as a reality in the moment, not a deficiency from the past.

- *Nourish* it in whatever way you can, letting it lead you forward, not back.

I recommend that you keep your journal and all that you wrote as you worked with this book close at hand. You will need and want the reminders of what is most important, and you will be served by having your own wisdom right at your fingertips. Your nonnegotiables, your sacred needs, and your sexual sovereignty are soul treasures, and they will guide you on a path that will make your experience of being a woman—and a sexual woman—a true gift.

Above all other things, and if nothing else "works" in any given moment, I invite you to choose gentleness as your default approach with whatever you experience. As you move ever closer to fully realized sexual sovereignty and to intimacies that are respectful, honoring, and right for you, it's crucial to also remember that the terrain of sexuality is a messy one. It can only be traversed and learned through experience, not just watched and figured out in a tidy way from afar. You and I and pretty much everyone have had one or many sexual relationships that were far from honoring, far from what we know and desire to be possible. As you grow in the direction of greater self-respect, self-authority, and sexual maturity, look back on who you were before with a loving gaze, not shame. All you or I or anyone is doing is learning the best and only way there is to learn—through experience, joy, hardship, complexity, and time. We are all, in an essential way, doing the best that we can. Entrapment in past relationships—and liberation from that entrapment—*this is our path*. We all walk it, and we become deeper, wiser women as a result.

Your deep feminine being was made to flower in the presence of love, care, cherishing, and sweet partnership. She was also made to temper in the fire, to recover, to resurrect, to transform and recreate herself. You may have lost touch with it in the past, but I hope you are sensing now that as a woman you were made for all that you will face in this life. Life is not perfect and it is not a fantasy: it's so much better than that.

Sexuality is a journey like any other life journey. Getting lost down dead-end roads, falling into holes, walking too long with an unworthy companion—all of this happens. It might not be awesome, but it's okay, and I promise you that no matter what you can rise above. The practices in this book are ancient in origin, but forever new, forever here for you. You contain the feminine wisdom of the ages, alongside the ever-renewing spirit of the present moment. You were made for this, and all you have to do is remember that and choose it.

There is a current rising in our world, and each of us is a part of it. This current is the upsurge of an experience of womanhood honored and respected for the full spectrum it encompasses. You are made of emotional tides, sexual currents, spiritual lights, and so much more, all existing together, all affecting each other. As you initiate into greater power and self-knowing through the trials of past lovers and broken intimacies, you are opening the door to a mystery that has no end. Your capacities are beyond imagining. Your radiance is forever renewing. Your heart is an eternal gift of beauty to the world and to any partner you find worthy to share it with. I stand with you, for you, and behind you as you walk the unique journey of womanhood that only you can walk.

Acknowledgments

I am ever devoted to the wellspring of deep feminine wisdom that called me to Her and blesses my every moment.

Deep love and gratitude to the women of grace and power that never let me forget who I am and who carried me through the journey that inspired this book—Sarah Byrden Deonesea LaFey, Jasmine Patten, Jamila Suzanne, Grandmother Lorindra, and countless others, unnamed but close in heart.

I bless the men who have been my initiators and who have written this story of power with me.

Gratitude to my sweet Paul, for teaching me what it is to love a tender King. And to Isaiah, who teaches me the ways of the Mother by being my sweet, strong son.

I love you mom and dad and Brandon, for lovingly enduring the decades of transformation and logically inexplicable choices that have paved my path as priestess.

Huge gratitude to Randy Davila and all the staff at Hierophant for patiently and expertly helping my words find their way into a simple, clear voice. It has been a miracle and such a grace to be acknowledged and mentored by you all.

And for all the women of Her Mystery School and beyond who have trusted and followed the love in my voice to remember their way Home, may you be forever blessed in all the ways that She blesses.

About the Author

Jumana Sophia is a deeply trusted teacher, beloved ceremonialist, writer, healer, and ordained priestess. She is a guide. She has raised two temples and founded Her Mystery School—an international women's ministry and mystery school.

Her work articulates the soul road of womanhood and the nobility, the eternal rightness, and the incorruptible beauty of female sexuality.

When a woman rises, all of life rises with her.

www.jumanasophia.com

Hierophant Publishing
8301 Broadway, Suite 219
San Antonio, TX 78209
888-800-4240

www.hierophantpublishing.com